GERI'S JEWELS & GEMS

GERI JEWELL

FOREWORD BY NORMAN LEAR

GERI'S JEWELS & GEMS

GERI JEWELL

GERI'S JEWELS AND GEMS | GERI JEWELL

Published by Core IQ Press

Photo credits: Christopher Volker, Pexels, Unsplash, Michael Jacobs, Sunny Bak, and provided by the author.

ISBN: 979-8-9902081-0-0 (Hardcover)

Printed by Book Printers of Utah in China.

Book design by Firewire Publishing

DEDICATED TO CHET COOPER,
EDITOR OF *ABILITY MAGAZINE*

CONTENTS

FOREWORD

BY NORMAN LEAR

I met Geri Jewell when she performed at the 2nd annual Media Access Awards in Beverly Hills. She wore her famous "I don't have cerebral palsy, I'm drunk" T-shirt with a pair of blue satin overalls. Her comedy was magic and, of course, she got a standing ovation. After the show, Norman Brooks introduced me to Geri and I told her how much I enjoyed her show. I told her how funny she was, but added seriously, "You're way before your time!" Without missing a beat, Geri responded with, "So, wait a couple months!"

Later that evening, I ran into Geri again in a crowded elevator. Upon recognizing me, or so I thought, she said, "I'm sorry, what's your name again?" Everyone laughed and rolled their eyes, and someone yelled, "Norman Lear!" I smiled, and said "And don't forget it, kid, you'll be hearing from me again very soon!" Unbeknownst to me, she did not hear my name when introduced, because she not only has cerebral palsy, but also has 70% hearing loss. But that has never stopped Geri from going after her dreams.

A few months later, I offered her the role of Cousin Geri on our NBC sitcom, "*The Facts of Life*." At the time, the show was struggling and NBC had reservations about its future. It had been canceled and then brought back with a smaller cast. Cutting the cast in half was done to allow greater character development for those who remained. This second season of the show was going to determine whether it would succeed or fail. The almighty Nielsen ratings were monitored each week for approval from viewers.

The very first "Cousin Geri" episode was written by Ann Gibbs and

Joel Kimmel and was taped about two weeks before Christmas in 1980. Upon airing, it received the highest Nielsen ratings to date, and the rest is history. I am so proud to have this rare jewel in my life, as she is the first person with a visual disability to be cast in a reoccurring role in a prime-time series on network television. Geri broke the glass ceiling and opened

IT IS THROUGH GERI'S PERSEVERANCE AND LOVE OF LIFE THAT ENDEARS HER TO HER AUDIENCE.

the door for people with disabilities on a grand scale. She has always seen her disabilities as blessings in disguise, and continues to be the life of the party, whether invited or not.

Since then, it has been wonderful watching Geri continue to rise. She has spoken at the White House on three occasions and before huge arenas, as well as having a groundbreaking role on the HBO series, *Deadwood*. We know that Geri is a talented performer, but behind the lights and crowds is a remarkable human being. It is through Geri's perseverance and love of life that endears her to her audience, and she continues to be a force to be reckoned with. She understands that disabilities are about the human condition. In life, our big challenge is facing our human condition. Geri has chosen to face her disability with class, dignity, and a big dose of humor!

Geri's Jewels & Gems is a gift to all of us all to see the wisdom and workings of a remarkable mind. With her unstoppable attitude, Geri shares a lifetime of insights of what it takes to go from being a "disabled child" from Fullerton, California, to becoming a performer, and knocking it out of the park in Hollywood, arguably the toughest businesses of them all. We are all better off for knowing Geri, and her book is a treasure!

PREFACE

On April 1st, 2011 my autobiography *I'm Walking as Straight as I Can* was published. And even though it was April Fool's Day, it was no joke, my labor of writing my memoir for the past year and a half paid off. It felt good that I was finally being recognized as a writer. After my book came out, I was asked to write a column for the *Huffington Post* as well as for *Ability Magazine*.

Although I did not write for the *Huffington Post* for that long, I did write for *Ability Magazine* from 2012 through 2017. I was grateful for this opportunity given to me by Chet Cooper, and once again I am grateful that he was willing to allow me to publish this coffee table book, featuring all of my columns that I wrote for the magazine.

Even though some of my columns are dated by content, the readers will be transported to life at that time, and therefore may bring back memories of their own from that same period of time, adding another layer of consciousness, looking back. We are always saying "Don't live in the past" but truthfully our past tell the stories we love to write and read about.

I am also grateful for Dr. Randall Bell's belief in me, and his assistance in publishing this book. I hope you enjoy these columns as much as I enjoyed writing them. I have also included personally picked photographs to complete my vision of a coffee table book. So grab your coffee and have fun perusing through *Geri's Jewels and Gems*.

—GERI JEWELL

HOLLYWOOD

GERI'S SURVIVOR GUIDE

Because I was on a sitcom called *The Facts of Life*, and because I know the actress Lisa Whelchel, I have received tons of e-mails asking me if I am aware that Lisa will be on upcoming episodes of the CBS reality series, Survivor. Well, of course, I was aware of it, and I support Lisa 100 percent. On another note though, I have been asked if I would consider doing Survivor as well. Truthfully, I thought of doing it quite a while back, and there are many directions we could go in.

For example, the show could feature only people with cerebral palsy—among others, RJ Mitte, Josh Blue and Tom Ritter. Again, we could broaden the spectrum and have the competition include all people with disabilities, although the athletes would have an unfair edge against those like myself. So, how could Survivor embrace people with disabilities and be totally fair?

Well, why not have six people with "real" disabilities compete against celebrities who have to simulate a disability and not sway from the disability that they have been assigned. For example, Heather McDonald would have to do her impression of "Cousin Geri"; Rush Limbaugh would have to have electrical tape across his mouth and one arm taped to his torso; Charlie Sheen would have to be blindfolded; Simon Cowell could only speak with a talking board and with one finger on each hand tapped down; Kris Jenner must wear a 200-pound fat suit and have no access to Botox; and Tom Cruise must be a wheelchair user and have no access to the Church of Scientology. Who would be the winner here? Probably Charlie Sheen, because even if he lost, he would no doubt spin it into a profitable self-marketing blitz.

Truthfully, those of us with real disabilities could easily out-survive these celebrities on an island any day, because the real winners in life are those of us who have always been survivors and are recognized for our abilities and not our disabilities. Those of us who are the real survivors in life include among many others: Michael J. Fox, Josh Blue, Marlee Matlin, John W. Quinn, The Push Girls, Stevie Wonder and Gabrielle Giffords.

All in all, winners in life do not see themselves as victims and know deep down that their greatest attribute is maintaining a positive attitude. The real disabilities in life are not the human conditions that challenge us, but the learned conditions that can destroy us: hatred, prejudice, abuse, deception, greed, hypocrisy, false pride and despair.

TO SURVIVE IN LIFE, WE MUST ALSO KEEP STRONG IN SPIRIT.

To survive in life, we must also keep strong in spirit. We cannot give up in the face of hardship. We must have compassion and empathy for others, as well as a good sense of humor. Because if we cannot laugh at ourselves and see the humor in any given situation, then we will become bitter. "Occupying bitterness" takes a lot of wasted energy; "occupying happiness" takes courage and perseverance!

RAISING THE HUMAN VIBRATION

For some reason, so many of us are going through horrific challenges. It feels as though the universe is throwing curve balls at an unbelievable speed, and just when we think we can come up for air, we are hit again. From what is happening globally, nationally or personally, none of us are spared in what we have to process on a daily basis. And yes, on top of everything else, Mercury is in that awful retrograde.

My heart is holding so many friends in a cloak of love, light, and spiritual strength. I am personally so grateful for all that I have been given in life... especially for the challenges and pain. Why? Because it has allowed me to feel compassion and love for others. The gift of all pain is in the "present" of feeling it so that we can heal and help others to do the same.

For those who do not care or feel genuine love for others, they're equivalent to a new car, running on empty. It may look beautiful on the outside, but on the inside it is an empty vehicle going nowhere. Sometimes the best thing we can do for ourselves when we are struggling with our own pain, is to help others with their pain. In other words, getting out of "ourselves" and being able to help someone else actually is helping ourselves as well.

Unfortunately, we are living in a world that is screaming "ME! ME! ME!" And that is a part of the problem that we experience in finding solace for anyone. As soon as we are able to shift that "me" energy, then we will find our own pain being alleviated as well. For example, if we are overwhelmed by financial hardship, we can lend someone our time and listen to their concerns and pain (no $$ involved). This allows our heart and mind to be in a "giving" way, rather than "taking" and feeling broke and worthless.

SOMETIMES THE BEST THING WE CAN DO FOR OURSELVES WHEN WE ARE STRUGGLING WITH OUR OWN PAIN, IS TO HELP OTHERS WITH THEIR PAIN.

When we take the time to help others, we lessen our sense of hopelessness. I've noticed on social media that a lot of people are sick of hearing "you are in our thoughts and prayers". And it is not necessarily because they do not believe in God or the power of prayer, but rather that it excludes ourselves from doing anything further to solve the problems or alleviate the pain. So, if we are going to pray for someone, lets also pray that each of us are given the awareness of what we personally can do to help others as well.

Praying for others is a way of asking God, or the universe, or the higher power to care for the person or situation we are praying for. However, if we are not willing to do our own part to truly care (and sometimes taking formidable action), then our prayers do not really carry the belief that anything can actually be done.

In the process of raising the human vibration, we must daily seek awareness in what each of us can do in raising the "human" condition. We may not be able to cure the cancer that a friend has, but we *can* call them, bring comfort to their journey. We may not be able to save someone's home from going into foreclosure, but we CAN help them to look into options and give them emotional support.

WE MUST DAILY SEEK AWARENESS IN WHAT EACH OF US CAN DO IN RAISING THE "HUMAN" CONDITION.

Also, we cannot turn the clock back and bring back all the lives that we lost in the senseless shooting, but we *can* seriously look at our gun laws and make a real effort to lessen the violence that we face on a daily basis. In shaming the students for the marches, we are truly in denial of the pain and suffering, and all we care about is ME ME ME.

For me personally, I was raised to believe that God helps those who help themselves. So if I really expect God to help me in life, I must help others in life in any way that I can. Being there for someone else opens doors and pathways. Being there for only ourselves and our own needs will not open any doors, pathways or even windows. Let's all contribute to raising the human vibration—do something, anything, in helping someone today!

HOPE & GLORY

I am among millions of people who was thrilled to see 2017 go bye bye. It was not a year that I will ever look back on and think, "Gee, I wish I could live that over again!"

Yet, even knowing this, I still find myself from time to time going back anyway: in my dreams, subconscious thoughts, or just through visceral blooms of pain, disappointment, and heartbreak.

However, it has occurred to me recently that every time I think of the struggle of those 12, soul-crushing months, I do go back and live it again, even though I claim it's the last thing I want to do.

So, how do we really recover and move forward from a bad year? I think the key is to become fully aware of what we focus on. By being in the now, we can stop ourselves in our muddy tracks, and shift internally to a positive, fresh path that changes our brain's patterning, allowing us to breathe more deeply and access natural joy.

For instance, if I am reliving the memory of losing my sister Gloria, who died of lung cancer in 2017, then reviewing that mental "snapshot" creates sorrow, detonating unhappiness, exploding into more unhappiness. Thus 2017 trails behind every step I take, even as I try to slip away from it.

Politics and other horrific events of 2017 have affected us all, challenged our faith, stirred our anger, and threatened our connection to positivity.

However, it's possible to catch ourselves in those thought processes and say, "No, I will not drag this negativity into today!"

I understand that many of us struggle with depression. For some, it's a biochemical reality deep inside our bodies. Fortunately, there are therapeutic measures to help us cope. And on top of that we have the power to stay aware, replacing difficult thoughts with affirming ones.

Many examples come to mind: A close friend watched her parents' brand new home burn to the ground one Christmas eve. The entire family stood across the street watching the house and everything in it, including newly purchased Christmas gifts, succumb to raging flames.

The trauma felt unbearable, until my friend's 4-year-old niece yanked on her dress and said, "Aunt Kelli, I know it's sad that grandma and grandpa lost their home, and all the presents are burned, but isn't it exciting though!"

The whole family laughed at her childlike innocence and later huddled together in a motel, celebrating that they'd all gotten out alive, where they unwrapped the real Christmas gift of life: they still had each other.

For me, my sister's death in 2017 was without a doubt the most painful thing I have ever experienced. And I have gone through the stages of grief, anger and despair. But as I move forward into the New Year, I make a daily effort to reach for the sweet memories of having Gloria as my sister, so they can take the place of any pain that tries to rise up.

I still laugh when I think of the day I was looking for an outfit in Macy's. I was hurting physically, and there were no benches or chairs to sit on, so I sprawled in the middle of the floor in women's formal dresses.

My phone rang in my purse, and it was Gloria. My hearing aides are synced with my iPhone, so as we chatted, it looked like I was talking to myself. She was telling me something excitedly, and I was sharing in her excitement and laughing.

Then a security guard came over and said, "Ma'am, you cannot sit in the middle of the floor. You have to get up, right now."

Gloria could hear him, but he couldn't hear her because her voice went directly into my hearing aids. She said, "Tell him to go f**k himself. You don't have to move anywhere!"

I said, "Gloria, I can't say that to him!"

He interrupts, "Ma'am, you have to get up. You cannot sit here!"

I said, "Gloria said I don't have to move."

He then thought I was talking to an imaginary friend, and replied, "Okay, you and Gloria can stay here, it's okay."

After that, Gloria and I couldn't stop laughing!

So as we continue to move away from 2017, remember not to take the agony of the old year into your new beginning. Make an effort to remember the good things and more will manifest. For me, 2018 will be one of magical hope and glory.

MAKE AN EFFORT TO
REMEMBER THE GOOD
THINGS AND MORE
WILL MANIFEST.

HOLLYWOOD

BOLD. BRAZEN. BANKRUPT.

We're living in a world where people who previously breezed by in the shadows, and at other times boldly marched the red carpet, are being revealed for who they truly are: morally bankrupt individuals.

Whether drugging women, molesting children, or otherwise harming others from their pedestal of power and prestige, they're now being outed by more and more accusers who bravely step forward to reveal their truths. These predatory conditions have always been a part of our society, but the instant nature of the information age has thrown the matter onto the hot seat of public display.

In spite of the number of accusers who have come forward, I suspect that some of those engaging in the behavior, who haven't been caught yet, will arrogantly continue to take their chances, which is horrible and distressing.

As they come to the surface, all of these breaches of trust—known and unknown—harm us in one way or another. This is why we must be extremely careful about how we respond. Rather than ricochet from headline to headline, we need to navigate the process in a way that we learn from it, and yet avoid becoming totally consumed by it.

I am by no means denying the disgust that we naturally feel, but suggest that after we honestly acknowledge the ugliness, that we take the steps to fight against it in the future and continue to embrace joy.

Remember what Martin Luther King, Jr. said: "Darkness cannot drive

AFTER WE HONESTLY ACKNOWLEDGE THE UGLINESS, WE TAKE THE STEPS TO FIGHT AGAINST IT IN THE FUTURE AND CONTINUE TO EMBRACE JOY.

out darkness; only light can do that. Hate cannot drive out hate, only love can do that." King was correct, and his wisdom also applies to tending to our individual pilot lights, which we can never allow to burn out, even as those who come forward to report these crimes, and those protest against them, whether massing in the street, or taking to social media to express their feelings, also face no shortness of criticism.

As I write about this, I feel deep stirrings of its effects on me, too. This year has been, without question, the most painful and challenging of my life. Surviving it, and learning to adjust my wings and sails to the enormous ever-changing winds, is a testament to my own ability to keep my little boat afloat, even when the wind of moral bankruptcy has tossed me around like a tiny boat upon the ocean.

I have faced anger and feelings of mistrust to the point that even my belief in a higher power has gotten shaken up from time to time. However, by acknowledging my own experience, I can make peace with the reality of it, and find some calm in the storm each morning by breathing and making conscious choices to love life and move forward.

We all do this in different ways. Sometimes I see messages on social media like: "The worst feeling in the world is being used and lied to" or "Such a disappointment when you defend someone for so long, thinking they are different, and they turn out to be just like everyone said."

People share these feelings publicly for many reasons. Sometimes they seek to create empathy for our pain, cathartic healing, or even to communicate to the actual person they perceive as causing the pain. These posts are usually followed by: Agree and share.

While I do support their self-expression, I rarely share these posts because they put the painful energy on display. I do usually acknowledge them, though, by sending a virtual hug or love, as a way to remind the person and myself that—if no laws were broken—it's best to forgive and let go, otherwise we get so caught up in our rage that it becomes our "fuel to exist" rather than our "light to live." The effect of that is to give the person in the situation the power to continue to snuff out our spiritual pilot lights.

Sometimes there's a fine line between the two energy fields of giving a voice to our pain, and soldiering on. We must stay aware of how we feel to keep ourselves balanced as we ease through the chaos and continue on our journey.

> IT'S BEST TO FORGIVE AND LET GO, OTHERWISE WE GET SO CAUGHT UP IN OUR RAGE THAT IT BECOMES OUR "FUEL TO EXIST" RATHER THAN OUR "LIGHT TO LIVE."

The best defense against those who would do us harm is to love and respect ourselves, to be there when others need us, and to consciously make choices that support the highest good of all with a sense of gratitude for life.

If we can embrace our blessings daily, especially during the most challenging times, we will prevail and show others what is possible, which can have a ripple effect of global proportions.

HURRICANES, FIRES & EARTHQUAKES, OH MY!

Lately, it seems as though hurricanes, fires and earthquakes are happening simultaneously around the world. It's as if Mother Nature has a serious bone to pick with us, and has unleashed her fury.

Some say it's the Lord's way of punishing us for doing wrong or, as one well-known celebrity put it, "God sends hurricanes to make sinners repent."

I, on the other hand, don't believe that Mother Nature or God have tempers. Anger is a human emotion triggered by perceived injustice. Visited upon others, rage can be toxic, cruel, selfish, and lead to fatal results. Because natural disasters seem to mimic the out-of-control feelings that fuel anger, we try to find someone to blame when Harvey floods our houses, Irma tears the roof off of an island nation, or tens of thousands of beautiful acreage vanish in flames.

Mother Nature is not trying to tear us down; she's quietly hoping that we hurry up and get our act together, so the planet survives and keeps spinning amongst the others in the universe, so we don't end up like one of those death stars that burns itself out.

From the time our planet came into existence, Mother Nature has patiently rejuvenated herself against whatever chaos we throw at her. We could go back to the Biblical flooding, but let's not. Instead, let's take a look at what we, as humans, do in the current era to bring these natural disasters upon ourselves, and join with the millions of people who are consciously paying attention to the ways in which we can assist our dear Kamacite.

Mother Nature does not care one iota about politics, religion, race, or sexual orientation, she hangs out amid the rainforests, the oceans, the ozone layer, and the polar bears, trying again and again to work her magic so we can remain healthy and thrive.

The wastes that we humans have created for centuries have wreaked havoc upon her land, water and animals. She's only trying to survive the toxicity we visit upon her. Instead of getting all worked up over a perceived blame game, the people of the world can accept that we're all in this together, and stop doing things that undermine Mother Nature's efforts. For instance, discarding so many plastic bottles for her to absorb; dumping bio-chemical poisons in her waters; fracking (and cracking) the earth, while aiming nuclear missiles at one another across the miles.

Truth of the matter is that every little bit that each of us can do towards making our planet healthier, lessens the drastic measures Mother Earth must use to right the imbalance we, ourselves, have created. What you can do about it: Sign petitions to stop fracking; give to the preservation of the rainforests; plant trees and flowers; and remember to recycle; these are the ways we can show our respect for Mother Earth and demonstrate our worthiness for her continuing hospitality.

I BELIEVE WE CAN ALL LIVE IN GLOBAL HARMONY, BUT WE MUST RID OURSELVES OF LAYERS OF DESTRUCTIVE PATTERNS.

Yes, I believe we can all live in global harmony, but we must rid ourselves of layers of destructive patterns. Our sacred planet suffers from the same cancers we find in our own bodies. In order to heal ourselves, we must love one another and the planet unconditionally, and treat this Earth as if we intend for future generations to live here. Because if Mama's not happy, nobody's happy.

BE COUNTED

For nearly four decades, I've been a stand-up comedian. I began honing my craft in 1978, inching out into the spotlight on clubs' amateur nights. I found that people can be uncomfortable with letting go and laughing; they tend to think that you're supposed to take life seriously, so I put them at ease by walking them into my world. I made it okay to laugh with me about the quirks of having cerebral palsy. I boldly put myself in their faces to be loved, hated, criticized, ridiculed, respected, adored and/or resented.

When we comedians step out on stage with a new audience before us, we never know how we'll be received. And yet it's just like exercising any other muscle; it becomes stronger the more you work it. Now truthfully some comics will never get stronger because, well, they suck. Their "funny" muscle is forever skinny, and they should probably stop now and look at becoming an accountant or a proctologist.

I can go onstage, flex the funny—pouring sweat at times when I've got a tough audience on my hands—and nail it. On those nights, I walk offstage, feeling good about myself. Other nights, not so much.

Everyone says it takes a lot of courage to do stand-up comedy. Perhaps so, but for me, personally, there's another "stand-up" skill that has been harder to master, and that's standing up for myself in life:

Having the courage to confront those who dismiss me, take advantage of me, and devalue my presence.

There's no stage or gym to work on that. This kind of stand-up muscle takes facing up to situations or people who go against my self-worth, belittle or bully me into feeling that I'm powerless, or not deserving of what I want in life, and what should rightfully be mine.

I've always had difficulty in this area, fearing anger or hurting someone's feelings. I can become passive aggressive, and beat myself up, instead of being honest, relaying how I feel, and going after what I really want. And I can assure you, being mealy mouthed in this way does not work ever.

Each time I fail to stand up for myself in life, the universe creates situations for me to try it again. At age 60, I'm challenged, more than ever, to get as good at standing up in life as I am at stand-up comedy. It is probably the most important lesson I'll ever learn.

If you read my autobiography, *I'm Walking as Straight as I Can*, you know that I was taken advantage of time and again, and paid a huge price for not developing my stand-up muscles early on. I hope that you'll forge the courage to stand up for yourself today and every day. You may be surprised how strong you become. Go on! I double dog dare ya!

Oh, and by the way, you can also have a sense of humor in standing up for yourself, as well. For example, I was once left in an airport in a locked wheelchair for a couple of hours. I couldn't walk well that particular day because I was in too much pain. I needed to use the restroom, and no matter how I tried to get someone's attention, I couldn't.

When I couldn't wait any longer, I placed my carry on in the chair, and pushed it from behind. When I returned to the gate, people were smiling. I smiled back and said, 'Sometimes you just have to be creative to achieve your goals.' Everyone laughed.

THERE'S ANOTHER "STAND-UP" SKILL THAT HAS BEEN HARDER TO MASTER, AND THAT'S STANDING UP FOR MYSELF IN LIFE: HAVING THE COURAGE TO CONFRONT THOSE WHO DISMISS ME, TAKE ADVANTAGE OF ME, AND DEVALUE MY PRESENCE.

FOCUS ON THE POSITIVE

In looking at the world today, I recognize that it's not the same world that my parents experienced, or even the one I remember growing up.

Too many people lack compassion for those who are different—be it another ethnicity, race, religion, disability, sexual orientation, or class.

In some ways these prejudices have always existed, but in the last three decades there seemed to be more tolerance for diversity as a whole. Or perhaps the bigotry was simply more hidden or glossed over. However, from the 2016 election on, there's almost been a tacit support of people expressing their prejudices, and with no apology for doing so.

From the 80's through 2012, Fortune 500 companies—as well as government agencies—invested in diversity and sensitivity training to create a more inclusive work environment. Not to say that these measures aren't still being taken, but it seems that far fewer strides are being made to uphold these values than in previous decades.

Meanwhile tolerance, in some cases, has devolved into resentment. Truthfully, I have always felt that "tolerance" is thinly veiled resentment in some ways. I mean, I've been tolerated many times in my life, and believe me, I can feel the difference between that and truly being accepted as equal.

THE NUMBER ONE RULE IS TO NOT ALLOW OURSELVES TO BECOME BITTER AND ANGRY.

So in understanding that we have become a less tolerant world, what can I do to help change it, and make it more loving, respectful and kinder to all?

Without going into politics, I would rather tackle our own individual worlds within the bigger world: What I can do is make a small contribution daily towards promoting positive energy, which creates a ripple effect throughout the world.

The number one rule is to not allow ourselves to become bitter and angry. Even when things seem negative, we must focus on the silver lining surrounding the situation.

For example, the other night I got all dressed up, put on makeup, gassed up my car, and drove to Beverly Hills to meet up with friends for a fun evening. I ended up waiting for almost an hour in the wrong location as I'd taken the address down incorrectly. Later I drove home, removed my makeup, and put my jammies on, feeling very depressed.

My roommate Alex came in and was curious why I was back so soon.

Instead of counting the night as a total loss, he looked on the bright side: "Well, you got dressed up, got out, and that excited you. Since your sister Gloria passed away, you've been grieving, and haven't been motivated to go out and have fun, so tonight was a good start!!!"

I took what he said to heart, and he was right: I needed to focus on the good that came out of it, not the pain and frustration of what felt like a wasted effort. Before I went to bed, I glanced at Gloria's framed photo on my dresser, and felt like something in her eyes affirmed that Alex was right, and to keep moving forward, knowing that she would be with me always.

"Remember, I always loved to laugh, and passionately embraced life," Gloria seemed to be saying. "And I can still do that through you. Buck up and don't lose your smile or passion for each and every day!"

As we contend with the issues of the day, we have to monitor our mental sandbox lest it become a litter box.

WE HAVE TO MONITOR OUR MENTAL SANDBOX LEST IT BECOME A LITTER BOX.

DAD ON AISLE 7

Like millions of other Americans, grocery shopping is frequently a part of my weekly routine. I do it independently, and there's a certain comfort in that. For example, knowing that I have enough money to grocery shop feels good, and a well-stocked refrigerator and cupboards mean that I can rest assured that I'll have something to eat when I'm hungry or thirsty.

The experience of going to the market also evokes fond memories of tagging along with my Dad on food-shopping excursions when I was a kid. Memories of him and my sister accompany me down every aisle as I reflect on how my father approached this Saturday-morning chore.

First of all, I believe he had undiagnosed Obsessive-Compulsive Disorder (OCD), because he had a system that had to be followed the same way every single time, and he never wavered from it:

He made his grocery list, and checked off each item as it was placed in the cart. That, in itself, wasn't odd; but if Gloria and I spotted something that we wanted, and it was not on his list, he wouldn't let us buy it. However, he'd write the items down for consideration for the next list.

Dad religiously cut coupons, and tended to choose the option that was less expensive over the one that tasted better, which undoubtedly came out of his growing up with six brothers in Buffalo, NY, during the Great Depression. In fact, for most of my childhood, we ate canned vegetables over fresh or even frozen ones. A lot of the time our meals consisted of what his mom or my moms' mother made—food that was cheap and could go a long way. We always had leftovers.

FORTUNATELY DAD WAS CHARMING, SO HIS QUIRKS WERE MET BY MORE SMILES THAN GRIMACES.

In the store, he'd start down aisle 1 and proceed to aisles, 2, 3, 4, and onto to every aisle in order, until he'd hit the last one. There was no skipping ahead, even though there might not be anything on an aisle that was on his list.

Everything would have to be placed in the cart a certain way, and at the checkout counter, the items had to be bagged the way that Dad wanted them bagged, even if it meant him showing the clerk how to do it.

Fortunately Dad was charming, so his quirks were met by more smiles than grimaces. In some ways, I'm like my father, only I've never made a shopping list in my life. I keep it in my head, and yet rarely return home having forgotten anything.

I know exactly what I'm going to get and, like Dad, I rarely waver from my mental list. I use electronic coupons stored in my phone, and I request that things be bagged a particular way. While I don't correct the store clerk when they get it wrong, I'm quietly annoyed when it's not done the way I want it.

Once I'm in the car on the way home, I feel a sense of comfort in having spent the last hour or so with my Dad. I know that he probably rolls his eyes when I unpack two bags of gummy bears and a pint of chocolate ice cream, but at least I do get some Malt-o-Meal and yogurt to balance out the junk.

The only thing that would make my grocery shopping any more comforting is for stores to have a call button in each aisle, so that an employee can come to my aid when I need to reach something that's too high on a shelf. Dad never had that problem, because he was well over 6 feet. I, on the other hand, am only 5'3". I usually have to stand there waiting for someone tall to happen by, and usually they do.

Sometimes I wonder if Dad spiritually sends them over. I wonder if he whispers into their ear from the Great Beyond:

"Hey, go over to aisle 7, my daughter needs some help with that bottled water on the top shelf!" And then I look up, and my angel has appeared.

BIONIC HEARING

As most of you know by now, I'm female, a fan of David Cassidy, and a person with cerebral palsy (CP). What you may not be aware of is that I've had significant hearing loss. In some ways, being hearing impaired has caused me more problems than CP. At least with the latter, it's not a hidden disability, whereas hearing loss is invisible, and can cause lots of misunderstandings.

Having both CP and hearing loss has caused even farther-reaching miscommunication in my life. For example, the line between what could "possibly" be a CP issue and what is a hearing-impairment issue becomes murky as they naturally overlap.

If I am not "responding correctly" is it because I didn't hear the information right? Or is it because I didn't developmentally process the information? Because my hearing loss is "hidden," often it's assumed that it should be chalked up to CP, when in actuality it shouldn't be.

An example: If a person asked me something simple like what is my address, I might answer: "I really do not like dresses all that much, and prefer jeans or a nice pantsuit." If you didn't know that I was hearing impaired, you might think: She's nuts!

Now add "celebrity" to the "CP" "hearing loss" equation, and there's yet another aspect to an already long list of assumptions. Example: "Miss Jewell, there is a fan in the other room, could I bring him in?" My answer: "How sweet, but I really don't need one right now, but I would love a bottled water. Thank you!"

One time, the L.A. Times reviewed my stand-up act at the Comedy Store even though I had only been performing for roughly seven months, so you can imagine how excited and anxious I was at the time.

The article gave me a rave review. However, there was one observation that cracked me up. The writer wrote: "This young girl is refreshingly funny and different, joking about having cerebral palsy. In fact, for being so young and new at her craft, she astounds me with her level of self-confidence, completely ignoring her hecklers, moving effortlessly into her next bit, leaving those who tried to bully her sitting sullenly. Her audience applauds Jewell's unwillingness to engage, and not allowing anyone to throw her off."

If truth be known, I didn't know I had any hecklers, because I never heard them!

Well, I am thrilled to announce that those days are gone!! I was so blessed to be introduced to Bill Austin, the owner of Starkey Hearing Aids in 1984. My hearing loss has been a challenge to correct for a number of reasons. I always needed a lot of power, and combined with the movements from CP, there were always additional concerns. For example, the ability to take them in and out, replacing batteries or wearing the devices comfortably without feedback, has always been problematic and frustrating.

IF TRUTH BE KNOWN, I DIDN'T KNOW I HAD ANY HECKLERS, BECAUSE I NEVER HEARD THEM!

Technology keeps getting better and better, and my newest pair of hearing aids are absolutely amazing!

They're called Halo 2, and even though halos are usually reserved for angels, I am delighted to wear mine! I have not been this excited about something since I met David Cassidy in 1985!

The most awesome thing about them is that they're programmed to operate using a Bluetooth through an iPhone, iPad or iPod. The Starkey app is downloaded, and all I have to do is put the aids in my ears, pair them, and I am ready rock!!!

My hearing is now virtually uncompromised. I can hear as well as, if not better than most people. I feel like Jamie Summers on The Bionic Woman! I can hear sounds and conversations I was never able to before! I've always heard the phrase that sound travels, but never realized how far until I flew home from Minnesota where the Starkey Labs are based. I was sitting in coach, but I might have well been sitting in first class, because I could hear just about everything that was said beyond the curtain that separated us.

Thank you Starkey Labs and Bill Austin for taking such good care of me over the years, and for always being willing to keep me up to date with the newest and best technology in hearing instruments. If anyone should be wearing a halo, it would be Bill Austin, whose passion for life and hearing has changed the lives of millions of people worldwide. I'm one of them. Now if only I could get another series or movie. I said, NOW IF I COULD ONLY GET ANOTHER SERIES OR A MOVIE!! Hmm, I wonder if my agent is hearing impaired?

PRIDE IS PLEASURE ARISING FROM A MAN'S THINKING TOO HIGHLY OF HIMSELF.

— *Baruch Spinoza*

FALSE PRIDE

I've had cerebral palsy since birth, which most people perceive as a disability, but which I believe it has put me on a path of monumental evolvement and understanding of the human condition.

From my initial diagnosis at 18 months, to being placed in special education, being bullied and ridiculed by other children, and ultimately being discriminated against in the job market, I have repeatedly bumped up against what others perceive as my disabilities.

I've also been exposed to other people's perceived disabilities. People who are blind, deaf, wheelchair users… Those who have muscular dystrophy, autism, Down syndrome, Bipolar Disorder, HIV, AIDS, or cancer are often viewed as diminished and worth less.

In truth, these conditions are only disabling if you see them as such. This applies to those who have them or live with them, as well as those who don't, and are looking in from the outside. However, on any given day, any one of us could cross over by acquiring a life-altering disability.

We live in a physical world of challenges, but the real crippling disabilities in life are disabilities of the spirit, which have the potential to threaten our survival as humankind.

They include but are not limited to:

- *Hatred*
- *Envy*
- *Prejudice*
- *Loss of faith*
- *Bullying*
- *Despair*
- *Deception*
- *Hypocrisy*
- *Greed*
- *False Pride*

Most of us can identify with one or more of these disabilities in one way or another, but the one not everyone fully understands is false pride.

THE REAL CRIPPLING DISABILITIES IN LIFE ARE DISABILITIES OF THE SPIRIT.

We are more familiar with other false 'hoods like false security, false prophets, false alarms and false teeth. Each of these terms tells us that the thing being described is not the real deal.

So, what is not true about pride? Is not someone's pride and joy something to feel good about it? Our children can be our pride and joy. We can take pride in a hard-won victory, like graduating from college or finishing a grueling marathon. Feeling proud of our accomplishments gives us a wonderful rush, but when we are prideful for the wrong reasons, then that is false pride and it carries serious consequences.

The reason I have singled out false pride is because we are seeing a lot of it in our recent elections—during the campaign and after.

We witnessed it during the campaign where millions of people arrogantly believed that one candidate would win the election hands down. Then in the aftermath, we've dealt with more false pride in what has felt like the "winners" gloating, and the "losers" scrambling to understand how they bungled an election that they should have had "in the bag."

Many of us have come to realize that we took false pride in our nation's seeming progress in such areas as race, gender equality, and religious tolerance. We thought we were well beyond the us-and-them polarity of bygone eras.

True pride is only attainable when we do not bring harm and pain to ourselves or others. Unfortunately this election has opened a Pandora's Box of rampant false pride from all sides.

America hasn't been so divided since Civil War broke out between the North and the South in 1861. After our most recent, bitter campaign season, however, we are once again charged with coming together as a nation, showing respect for one another, and reigning in such disabilities of the spirit as hatred, bigotry and despair.

I am all for peaceful demonstrations and movement towards a kinder, more tolerant society. I understand the power in admitting the error of our ways, and becoming more tolerant of ourselves and others. That said, I firmly believe that what is at the root of all false pride is fear: fear of what others will think, fear of failure, and fear of losing our faith.

No matter where we are headed and what transpires, the 2016 presidential election has proven to be a catalyst in bringing to the surface the bigotry and racism that has always been here, albeit hidden and smoldering. We have an opportunity to show the rest of the world that America will not tolerate hatred, bigotry or bullying of any kind. As a certain First Lady affirmed: "When they go low, we go high."

IF WE LEARN TO REALLY TO LISTEN AND ACCEPT ONE ANOTHER, WE CAN GROW AND EVOLVE INTO BETTER HUMAN BEINGS.

We must ponder the flight of the American eagle and soar higher, gaining strength and perspective in overcoming disabilities of the spirit. America was built upon the Constitutional rights and liberty of all Americans. We're not there yet, but if we learn to really to listen and accept one another, we can grow and evolve into better human beings. And that is something we would all be proud of.

Pexels

REAL CONNECTIONS

It's 2015, and we live in a world where it's easier than ever to stay connected to loved ones. However, because there are so many different ways to communicate, sometimes we actually communicate less than we did before we were bombarded with all this technology.

Think about it...

Flashback to the 70's and 80's. If you were alive then, you probably only had a landline, a typewriter and a box of stationery. We called friends on the landline, and returned calls if we had an answering machine that recorded voicemail messages. If someone lived at a distance, we wrote them a chatty note or a long letter. We made lunch dates, dinner dates, dates for Sunday brunch...and sometimes if we didn't have a date, we'd go hang out at the discos until we found one!

It's not that we don't do those same things today— although it's pretty rare to send (or receive) a handwritten letter. But with all the ways we have to keep in touch with people, our brains are sometimes operating on circuit overload. Should I Facetime, Skype, Facebook, instant message, tweet, text, call or email?

Also, the method of communication that you value as intimate, someone else may perceive as cold and impersonal. For example, let's say that you love to send text messages, but the person you're contacting hates to receive them—preferring a phone call. This can hurt the relationship.

The thing is, with seemingly infinite ways

to stay connected, it's become easier to be in touch with more people than we ever thought possible. So now that we have a few hundred "personal" friends, whom do we really wish to be close to, and how do we create boundaries with those with whom we'd like a bit more distance? If we do not create boundaries, then we don't have the time to focus on the relationships where there is genuine closeness and intimacy. We're close to everyone, at once, and everyone is close to us.

ALLOW THE WORLD OF YESTERDAY TO BE A BAROMETER TO THE WORLD OF TODAY

Some of us, through our texts, tweets, Facebooking, etc., juggle hundreds, possibly even thousands of relationships. So we need to ask ourselves this question: If it were the 70's or 80's and, given the opportunity, would I save a message from this person on my answering machine, or a note from them that I received in the mail?

In other words, allow the world of yesterday to be a barometer to the world of today, giving us a healthy perspective on all these relationships that we cultivate through social networking. There are a lot of wonderful things that can come out of the current era, but only if we understand honestly who we are, and what we want in our relationships with ourselves and with others.

Even in playing online games with others, we create a relationship. That's another area in which I run the retro test: Would I invite this person into my home to play Scrabble in 1977? If the answer is "yes," I start another game. If the answer is "no," it may be game over. I know you might think I'm taking the spontaneity out of fun, instant connections, but I don't think so. I believe that having to wrangle so many "relationships," even connections to friends we were close to in kindergarten, can make us lose focus of interpersonal bonding. Try giving each relationship the "hallmark" of focus: caring enough to send the very best of ourselves. That, my friends, is a way for us to

TRY GIVING EACH RELATIONSHIP THE "HALLMARK" OF FOCUS: CARING ENOUGH TO SEND THE VERY BEST OF OURSELVES.

JURY IS OUT!

Recently I attended Wild Honey Orchestra's tribute to the Beatles' White Album. It was a wonderful concert and my amazing & talented friend Nick Guzman (who has autism) did a duet with Susan Cowsill! But that particular record wasn't one of my favorite by the Beatles. And song No. 9 on that album was just weird; I couldn't wrap my brain around it. But it does trigger a memory of when I was chosen for jury duty in 1993. An odd correlation, I know, but as I explain my one and only jury experience, you may come to understand why my thoughts traveled back to that July more than two decades ago.

Let me set the scene: I had just moved to Las Vegas, NV, in March, and by summer I had been summoned for jury duty. For years, I had been able to get out of jury duty because of my cerebral palsy and profound hearing loss. The court system never challenged my medical excuse, which was great because I really didn't want to serve. It wasn't because I don't believe in the justice system, or that I'm not a loyal American citizen. But I was terrified of hearing something incorrectly and jeopardizing someone's right to a fair trial. Emotionally it was just too difficult for me to take that risk.

As it was, I called the courthouse and said that I could not serve because I had CP, and that I did not yet have a doctor's note because I had just moved to town. I was then asked how CP prevented me from intellectually comprehending information. Does it affect you cognitively? I said, "No, but I am hearing impaired as well."

They told me, "Well, we are in compliance with the Americans with Disabilities Act (ADA) and can accommodate you," At that point, I was in sheer panic mode! For years, CP and hearing loss had been considered a valid reason for me not to be on a jury, but with the passing of the ADA I was suddenly expected to serve. I asked her how the court planned to accommodate me. She told me that they would have a sign-language interpreter. I told her that I had never learned sign language.

Then, out of complete fear and lack of all understanding of how the jury system worked, I stupidly added that I couldn't serve because I was a television actress, a comedian, a celebrity. This statement caused the woman on the line to pause. After an awkward silence, she asked me how being a celebrity prevented me from serving on a jury. "Well, what if the defendant gets convicted of a crime, and they recognize me from Facts of Life, and then targets me later?"

She calmly told me that I was no longer Juror No. 23, but Juror No. 999. I was afraid to ask her what exactly that meant. She also said that I was to show up at the courthouse on Monday and tell the judge everything that I had told her.

On Monday, Jurors No. 18, 19, 20, 21, 22, and me, No. 999, entered the courtroom. Not only was I recognized from Facts of Life, but everyone laughed! I was in the very back of the room, and could not hear any of the proceedings (my original fear confirmed). So I raised my hand, as I had in high school civics class.

"WELL AT LEAST I AM NOT JUROR NO. 666!"

The judge acknowledged me: "Just state your jury number and your issue."

I said I was Juror No. 999, everyone laughed again, and responding as a comedian, I said, "Well at least I am not Juror No. 666!" The judge pounded her gavel to silence the laughter; clearly she was not happy.

She asked the bailiff to bring me closer so that I could hear. He put me in a chair right next to the defendant! I was close enough to touch him! He looked at me, and out of nervousness, I smiled. He rolled his eyes. After the preliminary proceedings, I ended up being chosen as one of the 12 jurors! I was scared out of my mind. When the judge asked us one more time if there was a reason we couldn't serve, I raised my hand again.

The judge said, "Yes Juror 999, what is it now?"

I said, "Well, I'm flying to Colorado tomorrow. What if I don't make it back in time for the trial?"

She said, "When is your returning flight?"

"Sunday night."

"So how does that interfere with the trial on Monday?"

"There could be weather problems."

"In July? On a flight between Vegas from Denver? What weather problems do you foresee, Juror 999?"

"Clouds?" I said.

At that point I was told that if I didn't show up Monday morning, I would be declared in contempt of court.

On Monday the trial began, and the judge informed the court that because Juror 999 was hearing impaired and did not know sign language, that counsels were expected to repeat every question to me personally so that I could read their lips. The ADA was brand new, and the court was trying to abide by it.

My saving grace that Monday morning was a fire drill at 11 a.m. We didn't get back in the courtroom until 3:30 p.m., by which time the defendant and his counsel announced that instead of proceeding with a trial, they would take a plea bargain. We jurors were all released.

I still believe that some people are not capable of serving on a jury. For me, at the time it was because of my hearing loss. Sometimes I hear "WAWWAWA AND WAWAAWAWA." I wouldn't want someone like me on my jury, and I don't feel confident that I would be fair to all parties concerned for me to serve, period!

To this day, I still don't know what Juror No. 999 means. I even tried to Google it, but found nada. However intuitively I think it means that I was willing to make up anything and go to any extreme to get out of jury duty.

In actuality, I did not lie. It's just that my valid reason was not accepted. So you be the judge.

POWER OF TV

As a member of the Baby Boomer Generation, I've always said that television played an integral role in my development. Even when I was in the womb, I was influenced by it, according to my mom. Her favorite series while she was pregnant with me were *The Gary Moore Show* (with Carol Burnett), and *Your Show of Shows* starring Sid Caesar.

It's no accident that at 13 I had a pen-pal relationship with Burnett, and years later become a professional comedian myself. Then there's the fact that in '84 I worked with Caesar to develop a sit-com called Sid's Kid, where I was to play his daughter. Coincidence or not? From the 50's on, TV has been a staple of American culture. Though it's evolved from a grainy picture in a box with rabbit-ear antenna, to crisp HD images in a sleek unit mounted on the wall, TV has remained an extension of the world in which we live. Some people cannot even fall asleep without TV's sounds and images flickering through the night.

Back in the day, there were only a handful of TV stations, and they all signed off at midnight. The national anthem would play as the American flag waved, and then a high-pitched beep would sound—I don't know—to an Indian dart board(?) for the next six hours.

Anyway, for me the late 60's through the 70's, TV was my emotional outlet. I was often lonely and isolated, so the characters on the screen became my friends in the subconscious realm. I would watch Leave it to Beaver, relating to all of the Beav's adventures. Couldn't wait to tune in each week to the *Mary Tyler Moore Show* (and always wished I had a friend like Rhoda), or watch *All in the Family*, where I learned through Archie how NOT to be.

I LIKE HOW TV INFLUENCED GENERATIONS OF YOUTH TO OVERCOME DISABILITIES AND PURSUE THEIR DREAMS.

By the 70's, TV created a diversion from those dateless teenage years, and the cuties I had in my mind were John-Boy Walton and Keith Partridge. (Sorry, Brady boys; I never had a crush on you.) However, years later I did have a date with Blair's French teacher, Mr. Palmer on *The Facts of Life*.

I'm so glad I'm a boomer, and that TV had such a powerful effect on me, motivating me to carve out a career in that medium. I like also how TV influenced generations of youth to overcome disabilities and pursue their dreams. With programming now available 24/7, I wonder if TV would have had the same impact on me and my career, if I were a member of the current generation, Perhaps I just would have become a TV junkie and gone, instead, into selling televisions at Sears, or possibly teaching or writing.

Seriously, we can find anything we want at any time of day on TV. We can watch whatever our heart desires, from *Perry Mason* to *Happy Days* to *American Horror Story*, and so on and so on. With cable, the channels are infinite!!! The History Channel, The Travel Channel, and The Logo Channel (which runs marathons of *Facts of Life*)... Not to mention the

Pet Channel to amuse our fur babies, the Cooking Channel (you can tell by my cooking that I've never watched it), or even the Investigative Discovery Channel, stories 24/7 about solved and unsolved murders.

Today we live in a very different world, obviously. Not to say that TV can't have a positive influence on us. Of course it can, but with more than 2000 channels some of us get so engrossed in other people's drama—and comedy and horror and suspense—that we forget to turn off the TV and get more involved in our own lives. Remember, it's okay to own a TV, but it's not okay for a TV to own us!

FAREWELL KITTY

My sweet kitty, Harry, is in process of transitioning with cancer. By the time you read this, he'll likely have crossed over to the other side, free of pain and suffering, and onto cavorting with all my other kitties who have crossed over during my lifetime—far too many to mention here.

No matter how many times I go through the pain of losing a fur baby, however, I know I'll do it again. Not because it gets easier, but because of the unconditional love and joy that pets bring into my life.

For as long as I can remember, I have dealt with losing these four-footed friends who have become a part of the family. When I was a kid, these pets were my best friends, and as an adult they're my children.

Very rarely do our pets outlive us. In fact,

a friend of mine suggested that I consider getting a parrot next time, given that they have long lifespans—longer than most humans. For some people, that may be an option, but I've never bonded with a bird, with the exception of a parakeet named Pepe, and also Big Bird.

For those of you who have never had a pet, it might be a little difficult for you to relate to "bonding" with them. But it's no different than bonding with another human. Love is love, and for the sake of love itself, I've cherished every moment that I've been graced with Harry's presence.

I adopted him when he was 10, and knew that there was the possibility that he might acquire health issues. But from the minute I brought him home, I fell hard for this adorable love bug. He was already an adult when I got him, so all the toys that we'd buy to amuse a kitten were of no interest to him. (With the exception of a red light pen; he chased that beam all over the place!) So, without the diversion of toys and with his lack of interest in catnip, we became close even more quickly than I ever bonded to a new kitten.

Harry made up his mind within the first day that I was his new Mommy. From that initial night, he slept with me under the blankets, and I felt as if I'd known him forever. I believe we had been together in many lifetimes before. It's entirely possible, given that cats have nine lives.

After a mere three months, he developed his first health issue, supposedly after he ate a spider, and it poisoned him. He was inconsolable, cross eyed, and kept losing his balance. I remember the vet telling me, that this was possibly neurological damage, and that even if he lived, Harry might be like this for the rest of his life.

In a kind of numbed shock, I said, "So what you're telling me is that I may have a cat with cerebral palsy now? Then I said, "Well, the doctors told my parents the same thing about me, and they didn't put me down."

At that point Harry was transferred

to intensive care and on an IV for three days. I rang the doorbell of the hospital on this third night at about 11, and asked if I could see Harry. A little reluctantly, they let me in to be with him.

He recognized me immediately, even though he was still cross eyed, and kept falling down when he stood up. I sang to him and told him I loved him, and that whatever his fate, I would support him. But he also needed to know that extended hospitalization was expensive, and that my employment was sporadic. I prayed for all my spirit guides and fur babies on the other side to help him with whatever his little soul chose to do. The next morning the hospital called to tell me that I could pick up Harry, and that his maladies had all disappeared! That was almost three years ago! I feel so blessed that I didn't lose him then, and since then we've thoroughly enjoyed our time together.

Now as he struggles with cancer, we both know that our days together are coming to a close. As painful as it is, however, we trust that we'll see each other again.

"Harry Houdini" will escape from cancer, but he has no desire to escape from love. He'll live forever in my heart. And yes, my furry son, I would do it all again. Thank you, my sweet loving Harry, for spending one of your lives with me!

LOVE IS LOVE, AND
FOR THE SAKE OF
LOVE ITSELF, I'VE
CHERISHED EVERY
MOMENT THAT I'VE
BEEN GRACED WITH
HARRY'S PRESENCE.

TICK TOCK

I woke up recently startled by the fact that my deadline to write my next column for "ability" was that day! First I spent about 30 minutes or so eyeing a blank Word document on my computer. Then, unable to think of anything to write about I thought, 'Hey! How about some peanut butter toast!' So I shut my computer off and dashed off to the kitchen.

It was only after I had sticky peanut butter on my fingers that I realized I wasn't all that hungry. In truth, I was procrastinating so I didn't have to face that dreaded blank page. After I finished my toast—waste not, want not, right?—I headed back to the computer. It was getting late, and I felt the pressure mounting.

Then it hit me, I want to write about time. We're all affected by it, and we all know how many hours there are in any given day. However, we all have our own way of relating to it.

Some of us feel like there's not enough time in each day to do all the things we need to do, while others have too much time on their hands and spend it surfing the internet for hours, or vegging out in front of a wide screen TV flipping channels and not watching anything in particular as they numbly kill time.

Time can feel like an eternity or it can whip by in an instant, depending on what we're doing. If we're doing something we love like soaking in a hot bath, or dining with a friend, time races by. But if we're stuck in a long line at the DMV, or waiting on hold for a customer service rep, probably in some far-flung place like Bangladesh, it can feel like it's taking forever.

TIME CAN FEEL LIKE AN ETERNITY OR IT CAN WHIP BY IN AN INSTANT, DEPENDING ON WHAT WE'RE DOING.

How interesting that we either love or hate time, and that we spend a lot of each day obsessing about it. Seriously though, if time didn't exist, we would not be alive. Time is an earthly reality, probably put in place by a sage mastermind so that all of life did not happen simultaneously.

The lyrics to the Byrds' song, "Turn! Turn! Turn!" come to mind, particularly the way their voices harmonize on the lyrics:

A time of love,
a time of hate
A time of war,
a time of peace
A time you may embrace
A time you may refrain
from embracing...
I swear it's not too late.

Basically the song means that you can fit everything you need to do into one lifetime.

One of the ways we learn about what to do during our brief stay on the planet is through our dreams. You may go to sleep and then wake up from an epic dream where you flew to France, climbed a hillside, frolicked in the ocean, and topped it off at Disneyland. In real time, it would take days, months, possibly years to do all these things, yet you accomplished them in the handful of hours that you slept.

So whether we believe we have too much time on our hands or not enough, we still each have a 24-hour a day to work with. So time is not really the issue here, so much as how we perceive it, and how efficiently we use it.

Whether we're waiting in line at the DMV, or swooshing through our favorite ride at Disneyland, let's tap into our gratitude for every minute we're alive. The choice to live in the moment is a different way to bend the hands of the clock and comprehend the elastic, illusion of time. And it can be more fun.

TIME IS NOT REALLY THE ISSUE HERE, SO MUCH AS HOW WE PERCEIVE IT, AND HOW EFFICIENTLY WE USE IT.

A STICKY SITUATION

Yesterday as I was standing in line at the grocery store, I couldn't help but notice all the gum on both sides of the checkout aisle. This, while the person ahead of me piled more and more groceries on the conveyor belt. (I never knew a shopping cart could hold so many items!)

Instead of becoming frustrated that I'd gotten in the wrong line, I focused on all the colorful varieties of gum on both sides of me. This also kept me from getting engrossed in Kardashian-related tabloid headlines.

A visual scan revealed at least 30 different kinds of gum, if not more. That's when it occurred to me: Gum is big business because legions of people are passionate about chewing it!

For most of us, our adoration starts when we're kids, and is probably an extension of our pacifier, which we were completely attached to when, one day, Mommy and Daddy took it away and hid it forever.

Unlike hard candy, however, gum had a lot more rules associated with it:

- *We were never to swallow it because it did not digest like regular food, and someday we would bankrupt our family with an expensive surgery to remove the huge wad of gum blocking our small intestine.*
- *We could not chew gum in school.*
- *We could not chew gum in bed.*
- *We were not to stick it underneath our desk.*

- *We could not throw it out a car window.*
- *We could not chew it in church.*
- *We were not to use it to hang posters.*
- *We were not to crack it.*
- *We were not to chew the whole pack at once.*

These straitjacket-like rules seemed endless, and yet we still loved our gum! I personally loved Bazooka bubble gum the most because—in addition to blowing awesome bubbles—I got a comic-strip wrapper featuring the adventures of Bazooka Joe, along with my fortune at the bottom!

DON'T LIVE IN THE PAST BY CHEWING OLD GUM.

These days we have sugar-free gums, gums that whiten our teeth, and gums that freshen our breath. I mean, why do we even need a toothbrush or mouthwash or even a trip to the dentist for a cleaning? Apparently all we have to do is chew the right stuff!

I will be sticking with gum forever. Fortunately for us billions of gum lovers, the surgeon general hasn't come out with a warning that chewing it is hazardous to our health. In fact, many give up the deadly habit of smoking by switching to gum instead. See what I mean about the pacifier theory? We always have to have something in our mouths! (Get your mind out of the gutter; I made no reference to that. You went there yourself!)

In any case, as I scanned all the rows of gum at the checkout counter, I looked for my beloved Bazooka and determined that gum has something wise to impart to us:

One should only chew one piece at a time, and toss it once it becomes old and tasteless.

Don't live in the past by chewing old gum, and don't harbor it inside of you either.

Stick to your dreams, and never let anyone else burst your bubbles!

STICK TO YOUR
DREAMS, AND NEVER
LET ANYONE ELSE
BURST YOUR BUBBLES!

WIDE AWAKE

It is 3:30 am, and I am still wide awake. I went to bed around 11, but my mind won't turn off. I've thought of everything from my deadline for this column, which I have yet to finish, to my ex-husband, who popped up in my dream last night.

Did I remember everyone in my prayers? Is there enough water in my kitties' drinking fountain, and if so, did I remember to change its charcoal filter? Did I make all the right Scrabble moves?

After three and a half hours of racing thoughts, I've decided to write my column on the very thing that would not let me sleep: insomnia. I did briefly go on Facebook to see if any of my friends are awake, but there's no evidence of anyone being online. Besides, even if one of them were up at this hour, what would I say: "So, you're awake too?"

About 30 percent of Americans suffer from insomnia, a condition marked by difficulty falling asleep, staying asleep, or an inability to go back to sleep if one is awakened too early.

Although no one has ever died of insomnia, it

does affect one's quality of life. After a night of "Occupying Sleeplessness" one can be tired all the following day, and unable to be as productive as we could be. And we all know how dangerous driving can be when we're overtired.

Although we don't always know the cause of insomnia, we anxiously seek solutions. We take hot baths, drink herbal teas, and try to "veg" out to white noise. We wear sleep masks, count sheep (although I prefer to count penguins), and sip wine. Sometimes we even feel a need to bring in the big guns: prescription sleeping pills.

I've always had difficulty sleeping. When I was a little girl, my mom used to get so frustrated because she'd put me to bed at 8 pm, and I'd still be wide awake at 11. I think it was because my sleep in the womb was rudely disrupted by my traumatic and premature birth. So I might actually have post-traumatic sleep disorder—my own self-diagnosis, as I am not a doctor. Whatever it is, it all boils down to the same thing: difficulty sleeping.

I envy that my cats can curl up in a ball right next to me, and are sound asleep in minutes. Can I learn something from them? Probably so. They are not concerned with what is on Netflix, who will be the next President, or how much money they have in savings. They don't obsess about what their twitter password is, or if they have adequate health insurance.

IT REALLY CAN BE AS SIMPLE AS HAVING GRATITUDE, AND NOT OVERTHINKING EVERYTHING.

All they're concerned about is that they are the loved, that they have food and water, and that I know how much they love me. Their basic needs are met, and therefore they can easily drift off to sleep.

It really can be as simple as having gratitude, and not overthinking everything. But many of us become impatient with ourselves, and sometimes make things worse by harboring fears that tonight it will happen again: We'll be unable to sleep.

Perhaps, subconsciously, we tell ourselves that we need to stay awake in order to maintain control over a situation, or to keep working ceaselessly on whatever problem is keeping us up.

In the movie White Christmas, Bing Crosby sings, "If you're worried and you can't sleep, count your blessings instead of sheep. And you'll fall asleep." Again, there is power in expressing gratitude.

As I type the last few lines of this column, I am thoroughly grateful that I'm about to check this obligation off my list, and I shall celebrate that with a catnap right next to the kitties.

But before I nod out, I want to acknowledge a few more things that I'm grateful for: family, friends, and the good fortune to live my life to the fullest.

Awake, I can make a positive difference by doing for others, and asleep I can dream of infinite ways to better the world in which we live.

AWAKE, I CAN MAKE A
POSITIVE DIFFERENCE
BY DOING FOR OTHERS,
AND ASLEEP I CAN
DREAM OF INFINITE WAYS
TO BETTER THE WORLD IN
WHICH WE LIVE.

CRYPTIC MESSAGES

A cryptic remark has a hidden meaning and is understood only by those for whom it is meant. A cryptic code is a language system understood only by those who are familiar with the code. A cryptic reply is a very brief response conveying little and not plainly understood. And a cryptic message on Facebook, Twitter, or Instagram, is usually intended to send a specific message to one person, yet at the same time broadcast it to everyone.

If truth be known, I am probably the princess–if not the queen–of cryptic messages, although I do not believe I always was. As a kid, I basically took everything at face value. My first time around the rodeo, I never questioned if there was a hidden message or agenda behind what I perceived. It wasn't until high school that I began to detect that sometimes there were layers to messages, and began to wonder what someone or something really meant beyond what was being communicated. That being said, I can safely say that being able to add layers of meaning is a form of intellect acquired with maturity. Although some people don't "get it" and never will.

THE MORE WE DO NOT TRUST SOMETHING OR SOMEONE, THE MORE WE LOOK FOR WHAT MAY BE HIDDEN.

Something that can mean more than one thing requires a way of thinking that challenges our perceptions and forces us to look beyond the obvious. Babies do not come into the world and question their surroundings, like "Hmm, I wonder why my pacifier is pink. What does this really mean?" We're born trusting completely and this, in my opinion, is the hallmark of cryptic messages. In order to develop the skill, one must first experience lack of trust. The more we do not trust something or someone, the more we look for what may be hidden. I personally developed trust issues in high school and began to question more as a result, rather than blindly believe everything and everyone. This can be a good quality to have, if not taken to the extreme, where we destroy a sense of trust in all things.

Now let's jump to the use of social media and cryptic messages. Remember, this is a new medium and has the potential to reach hundreds, thousands, and even millions of people quickly. So this communication of sorts should be used with care, caution, and responsibility. The problem is we cannot always control what people put out there. Truthfully we can only control what we put "out there" ourselves, and how we respond to what other people choose to post.

Basically, we are all using social media to communicate something. Recently I posted on Facebook, "I am not going to write any sort of cryptic message here. Goodnight."

The next morning there were several responses like, "Hmm, I wonder what she really meant by that," and one specific one, "I understand–we'll talk tomorrow. Goodnight." To which I replied: "No, you don't understand because this post has nothing to do with you... lol, have a beautiful day!"

True, my post had nothing to do with the friend who thought it did. However, it was a cryptic message to another friend, who had posted a cryptic message, which I assumed was directed at me. Instead of responding directly to the original message, I just wrote something cryptic on my own timeline suggesting that I wasn't going to engage with the friend. But I still don't know if the original cryptic message was intended for me, or whether this friend has even acknowledged my cryptic message. The only thing that we achieved was to passive aggressively validate our feelings.

So what is the harm? In this particular case, there was none. However, if we are using social media to communicate a grievance with someone intimately, then we are doing harm to ourselves by bringing everyone into something that should be private. We therefore are using social media to validate or empower "our side of things" and passive aggressively expect our friends, colleagues, acquaintances (and sometimes even those we don't even know) to become allies, witnesses or therapists.

WE ARE ALL USING SOCIAL MEDIA TO COMMUNICATE SOMETHING.

This kind of communication is not really as harmless as we may think. Let's say a friend of yours RSVP'd but did not show up to your party and, instead of calling the friend, you write on Facebook, "There's always a party pooper or someone who found a better party to attend, but was a no-show at yours." The danger with these cryptic messages involves making assumptions. First, the assumption is that we've been wronged, and second that others will think this message has something to do with them.

Even something as innocent as posting a quote like: "I usually give people more chances than they deserve, but once I'm done, I'm done." If there is an unresolved issue with a friend, and they read that message, the issue may never get resolved. Better to wait to post something like this way down the line, long after any personal issues have been resolved. We need to stop using social media as "the couch" because all we are really doing is communicating passive aggressively, when there are qualified doctors, counselors, ministers, and close friends we can turn to privately. We can still write cryptic messages, but without the hurt feelings that can result from them. And yes, this cryptic column was about you...lol!

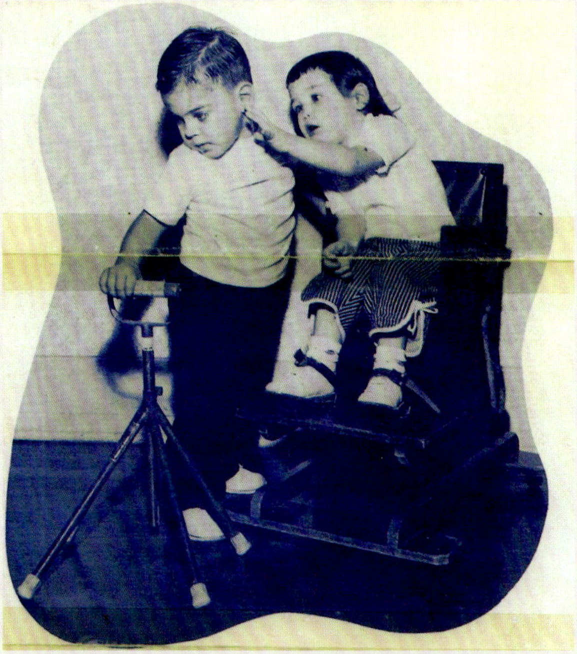

Geri as a poster child at age 2 with a classmate for AIDES, a charity for disabled children

Geri at age 13 with her sister Gloria

In Long Beach, Geri at the age of 2

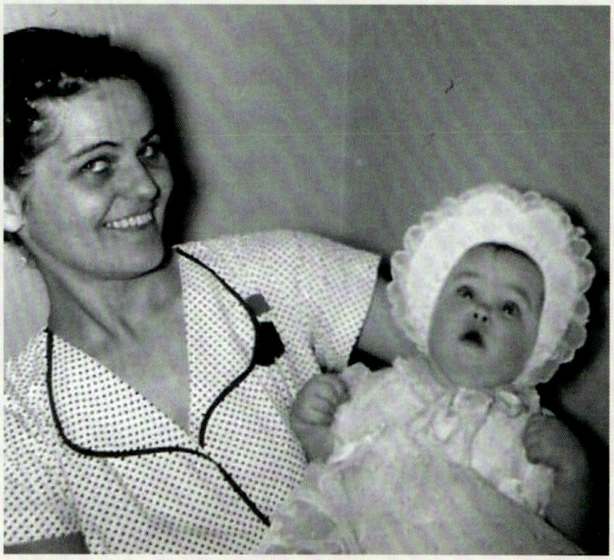

Mom and Geri as a baby in 1957

Geri and Gloria at the LA Zoo at age 9.

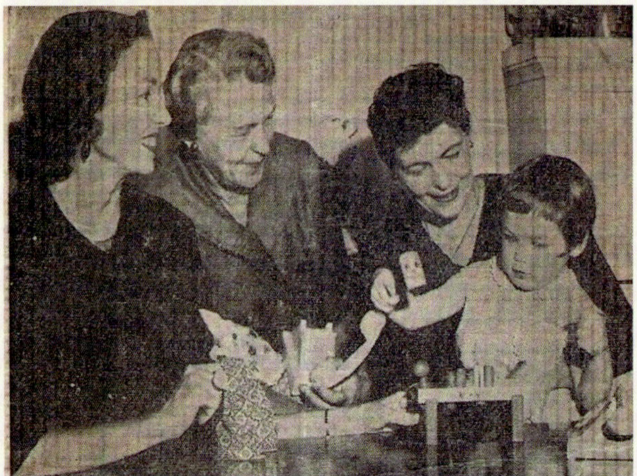

00 BIDDEN TO SUPPER-DANCE

Centering their love on children and their philanthropic efforts on aiding those suffering from cerebral palsy, Peninsula Committee of Spastic Children's League has issued 400 invitations to supper dance next Sunday afternoon in Petroleum Club of Long Beach as benefit for Seaside Hospital's United Cerebral Palsy Pre-School Nursery and Spastic Children's Foundation. Among patronesses planning event are (from left) Mrs. Robert Buffum Mrs. Wallace Ginder, dance co-chairman, and Mrs. Charles Holmes, league president, who holds Gerry Jewell, daughter of Mr. and Mrs. John Jewell 1020 Ohio Ave., a nursery school student.

Long Beach newspaper article on Geri at age 2 advertising a fundraiser

Geri and Dad at age 36

Geri riding her bike, a gift from Dick Clark in 1982

Full body shot of Geri at age 38

Geri, sister Gloria, and Flip Wilson in the Bahamas in 1988 at age 32

After Geri appeared on Sesame Street, Big Bird puppeteer Carroll Spinney presented Geri with this autographed photo

Bob Hope and Geri in 1983 at age 27

Geri performing at the 2015 Sedona World Wisdom Day Conference in 2015

Chad Everest, Geri, and a child with cerebral palsy for UCP event

Charlotte Rae and Geri in 1982

Halloween Costume from 1982 sold in the stores and voted as one of the worst 100 costumes in history

Scrabble game with Gloria, who put her name down on the triple word score to win her last game against Geri

...to be continued

David Zimmerman photobombing Geri's photoshoot

Norman Lear and Geri

On the red carpet for the Daytime Emmys in 2013

Paley Center in Beverly Hills Lisa Whelchel and Nancy McKeon 2013

Don't fuck with me!

Gloria and Geri at the Media Access Awards in 1994

Toby Forrest, Kathy Buckley, Michael Steiner, Mark Povinelli, and Geri for a promotional shot for *Perfectly Imperfect* in 2014

Deadwood promotional shot in 2019

Carol Burnett in 2014

Geri's favorite picture of her sister Gloria

Gloria and Geri in 2015

Juliet

Joey accidentally scanning his own butt

Sebastian and Geri

A VOTE FOR THE AMERICAN DREAM

This presidential election year seems more intense than any I've ever experienced in all my years of voting. And truthfully it's the only election in which I'm still undecided this late into the political season. Part of me is so disgusted with all that's happening in our country, that I feel a sense of dread and hopelessness. I wonder if my vote is even going to make a difference.

Though I lack excitement about any of the candidates currently in the race, I'll still show up and cast my ballot on Election Day, if for no other reason than to exercise my freedom and right to do so. As a woman with a disability who is gay, I must make sure that I'm counted and valued, and that my voice is heard.

I remember the first time I ever voted for our nation's leader back in 1976—40 years ago! Back then, I was so excited to register, and even though Watergate and the coverage of it on television created huge trust issues in politics (as the previously elected president had been impeached), I was still relatively innocent and believed, as many youth do, that we could overcome our difficulties and move forward to a greater America. Besides, I had dreams to pursue, and believed in my heart that my country would support me on my journey. In turn, I also felt honored to support my country.

I HAD DREAMS TO PURSUE, AND BELIEVED IN MY HEART THAT MY COUNTRY WOULD SUPPORT ME ON MY JOURNEY.

Today however, I'm a lot more somber than ever. I have lived a full life, and have realized so many of my dreams. I'm grateful for being a citizen of a nation that has given me so much freedom to be who I am, and to accomplish more than I ever imagined I could. What I did not expect, though, was to be struggling as greatly as I am at this point.

Honestly, even if I could, I would never choose to rest on my laurels by simply kicking back and enjoying my "golden years." I believe we should always strive to make a difference in the world. Now, more than ever, none of us can give up and close our eyes to what is unfolding right in front of us as these candidates crisscross America on the campaign trail.

I thought we were a nation divided during the last two presidential campaigns, but things have gotten even more divisive and scary in recent months. I am not telling anyone who to vote for, but I am encouraging us all to go beyond watching debates, and to stop being spun around by sound bites. Look deeper into what the candidates stand for, examine their leadership records, and know why you're voting for that person.

Even as we slowly emerge from the economic downturn (from which many of us are still far from recovered), we're weary of dealing with a broken political system that has forced so many of us to forget what the "American Dream" is about.

This nation's greatness is what convinced me, as an 18-year-old kid with cerebral palsy, to believe that I could be an actress and writer, and to actually go forth and make it happen. While there will be those who ridicule me for embracing peace and love, there will always be a bit of the "flower child" in me.

So many of us have lost our ability to believe in ourselves that we have resorted to the age-old tendency to find someone else to blame when we feel we can't achieve success. It's as if we have gone back 50 or 60 years instead of continuing to move forward.

The revolution back in the day happened for the same reason we're in our current quandary: The pursuit of happiness was not being supported on the bigger societal stage. And I will say that if we are unable to find happiness personally, we will never find it outside of ourselves.

Just know that whomever becomes our next President will not be able to create your personal happiness. That is only something you can do yourself, and it is something you must choose. As we take our individual power back, we will begin to experience the greatness America was built on. Our political system is what it is, and it needs to evolve, but positive change can only occur when it comes from within, first and foremost. Each morning we wake up, we must make a decision to sing in the rain or cry in the mud puddle.

POSITIVE CHANGE CAN ONLY OCCUR WHEN IT COMES FROM WITHIN, FIRST AND FOREMOST.

OPPORTUNITIES

Earlier this week I awoke with a massive headache at 4 a.m., but instead of trying to go back to sleep I stayed up and asked Spirit to guide me through the pain.

The throbbing at my temples was intense, but I'm wise enough to know that sometimes if we remove blockage in our spiritual realm, physical hurt will ease as well.

What I discovered that morning is something I've always known, but sometimes forget: There are no missed opportunities in life, it's just that not all opportunities are meant for us, like roles I haven't gotten over the years. That just meant they were someone else's blessing, not mine... So instead of feeling bad about something that didn't come my way, healing the sting is about feeling joy for the person who did get the opportunity.

Have you ever run to catch a train, only to watch the doors close and the train pull away? You stand there feeling frustrated and cheated? Trust that the Universe had a very good reason for you not being on that train! A friend's father sometimes reminds her: "People rushed to get on the Titanic."

THERE ARE NO MISSED OPPORTUNITIES IN LIFE.

As I lay there with my head hurting, I trusted that it could feel better. What came up for me was that I had not called my friend Ralph Richeson earlier. Granted, I had only heard, via a private Facebook message, that Ralph was in hospice care the night before. Still, I had every intention of calling him when I awoke. However, by the time I went online to get the phone number that was in the Facebook message, it had been updated and read: "Geri, I regret having to tell you, but Ralph passed early this morning."

I cannot tell you how horrible I felt that I hadn't called. However, during meditation a message came through that even if I had made the call earlier, I still wouldn't have been able to reach him. So I spoke with him that morning through a much better connection than Verizon could ever offer. I expressed to him that I was grateful for knowing him, and was thrilled that we actually had a scene together in the final season of HBO's Deadwood.

For those of you who are not familiar with Ralph, he is one of those rare background players who caught the creative eye of David Milch and became the eccentric, lovable character of Richardson, who resided at the Grand Central Hotel and had the oddest fixation with a deer's antler. If we had gone into the 4th season of

Deadwood, we probably would have had more scenes together. However, that wasn't meant to be. As I opened my eyes from my meditation, my headache had already begun to dissipate, making room for his beautiful presence. In my mind I saw his smile.

Although I didn't know him really well, we both shared the journey of appealing to David Milch's creative vision, and our characters were very similar in nature. Deadwood put both of us on the map, allowing a dream to come true for both of us in a different way. I guess in some ways we were both inspirations for the underdog. I only had one scene with him in the last season of Deadwood, and as with all of us, we were looking forward to a Deadwood movie, eventually.

The movie is back on the table, and may still be a reality, but there will be some actors who will not return because either their characters were killed off, or the actor didn't live long enough to be killed off. In any case, there are no accidents in life, and we all must be grateful for every day that we live, because another day is never promised...

Ralph, I raise antlers in honor of your eternal journey.

WE ALL MUST BE GRATEFUL FOR EVERY DAY THAT WE LIVE, BECAUSE ANOTHER DAY IS NEVER PROMISED.

PRESCRIBING LOL

Has a doctor ever given you a prescription for laughter? No? Too bad, because laughter may very well be the most non-toxic, life-altering drug we can get! It doesn't matter what's ailing us, whether it be cancer, diabetes, cerebral palsy, high blood pressure, or arthritis—laughter can help all those conditions. Not to mention other things that may threaten our well-being, such as unemployment, grief, traffic jams, and the tremendous confusion and stress of trying to wrap our brains around the Affordable Healthcare Act and other insurance matters.

The good news is that no matter what insurance policy you have, or what your deductible is, laughter is free! Yup, it's free, and if your doctor will not write you a prescription for it, then write your own. If you have to have a visual, then take an empty pill bottle, put a "laughter" label on it, and fill it with sugar-free candy. Every time you take a laughter pill, you must laugh for 10 minutes! Dosages may vary, but I personally recommend at least three "pills" a day.

Why? Because it will make you feel better, and that good feeling is highly contagious, so you'll help others feel better too! Laugh with your family, friends, colleagues and doctors. If this is not possible, then laugh all by yourself. You might even consider laughing with strangers. However, I do caution that your laughter be in good fun, no cruel jokes at someone else's expense. That will only prolong whatever ails you in the first place.

It might also surprise you that you don't even have to have a sense of humor to laugh, although it certainly helps. Laughter is a powerful healing tonic physiologically. The brain does not know the difference between a real laugh and a phony one—unlike a fake orgasm. When we laugh, the brain releases endorphins that ease the stress and pain we're dealing with. Truthfully, if I personally did not have a sense of humor, I would have given up a long time ago.

Recently I had to meet with a social worker about the daunting subject of health insurance and disability: HMOs, PPOs, who's covered, who's not, and what I needed to do to qualify. I was so overwhelmed that I was on the verge of tears, when all of the sudden I smiled and said, "Do you think Helen Keller had to deal with all this @*#&?" I laughed, the social worker laughed, and we both enjoyed the momentary comic relief and felt a tad healthier for it.

DO YOU THINK HELEN KELLER HAD TO DEAL WITH ALL THIS @*#&?

Bear in mind that the language of laughter is universal. Yes, we may not all laugh at the same things, but if anyone were to play a CD with only the sound of laughter on it, we would all "get it," find ourselves tickled, and join in.

When I was a kid, my whole family would often start laughing at the dinner table, and usually it was my older brother, Fred, who started it. If it was a particularly intense atmosphere—maybe my sister, Gloria, being forced to finish eating something she hated, or my dad being in a foul mood for no other reason than that fact that he was in a foul mood—Fred would cut through the tension by making faces when dad wasn't looking. Or he might take food off Gloria's plate in plain sight, and "hide" it under her plate. Even my dad could not help but laugh. It changed the energy at the table, and suddenly we were all giggling and enjoying one another's company.

Remember the line from the movie, Forrest Gump, "Stupid is as stupid does?" Well consider this: Funny is as funny does! And yes, funny does a lot of things— mainly give us a break from all the frickin' drama that can bombard us from all directions, blocking our innate childlike nature that delights in having fun. So don't forget to take your laughter medication three times a day and LOL.

FUNNY DOES A
LOT OF THINGS—
MAINLY GIVE US A
BREAK FROM ALL
THE FRICKIN' DRAMA
THAT CAN BOMBARD
US FROM ALL
DIRECTIONS.

SCRAPBOOK

SCRAPBOOK MIRACLE

As most of us have learned, there are pros and cons to Facebook (FB). But then again, there are pros and cons to everything under the sun. There are even plusses and minuses to the sun itself. Sure, it gives us warmth, light and Vitamin D, but if we don't make wise choices that heavenly star can also burn us by causing skin cancer, cataracts and wrinkles. But I'm not writing about the sun today; I'm writing about FB, and a miracle that happened because of it.

Actually, FB has been responsible for several miracles in my life. When I first signed on to the social networking site in 1999, I connected with Ted Nichelson, whom I previously did not know. We became FB friends and, as a result, got together and wrote a book proposal. That in turn launched the publication of my autobiography, *I'm Walking as Straight as I Can.*

Another FB miracle occurred when I connected with my first cousin,

Kelly Jewell-Basile. She and I had never met before, nor did I remember her mother, Phyllis, whom I last saw when I was 6 years old in Buffalo, NY. So when I accepted Kelly's friend request, I was blessed with a "new" cousin and aunt, and recently drove to Las Vegas to meet them. It was also a great opportunity to surprise my Aunt Phyllis on her 71st birthday. I cannot tell you how much joy and fun I had being a part of her special day!

IT WAS SUCH A MIRACLE TO HAVE A TREASURED SCRAPBOOK MAKE ITS WAY BACK TO ME AFTER 30 SOME-ODD YEARS.

Las Vegas is a city I know pretty well, as I lived there for six years. It's also a place with great pros and cons. Nevada has no state income tax; the buffets offer delicious and inexpensive meals; and the entertainment is magnificent. Yet there's the constant temptation of gambling, scorching heat in summer, and enough desperate energy to drag anyone down.

At the same time, it was from dazzling Las Vegas that my next miraculous FB event occurred. Jay Schwartz—again someone whom I did not know—sent me a private message, telling me that he had a scrapbook of mine, and would like to return it. I told him that I had no recollection of ever owning a scrapbook, but he said that he was sure it belonged to me, and uploaded photos of it as proof. When I saw the images, they jogged my memory.

I was so blown away and overwhelmed when I perused the photos of this long forgotten scrapbook that was stolen from me more than 30 years ago! Tears trickled down my cheeks as I looked at telegrams from Carol Burnett, Dick Clark, Brandon Tartikoff (then-president of NBC) and Johnny Grant (then-honorary mayor of Hollywood).

There was also my first contract from *The Facts of Life*, and sweet notes, cards and letters from my co-stars on the show: Charlotte Rae and Lisa Whelchel. There was even a letter from Barry Goldwater, several handwritten letters from comedian Bob Nelson; my contract from the film I did with Cheech and Chong (*Nice Dreams*); and so many other keepsakes from 1979 to 1984.

It was such a miracle to have a treasured scrapbook make its way back to me after 30 some-odd years, especially when you consider that it came from a gentleman who sold celebrity memorabilia to raise money for charity. There are not many people who would have taken the time to locate the rightful owner of such an item.

Jay mentioned that someone had brought the book to his store about 20 years ago, but after he had the opportunity to look through it more carefully, he realized that it was much too personal and decided not to resell it, and instead to return it to me. When he couldn't find me for several years, he put the book away in a filing cabinet. Recently, he rediscovered it, and decided to search for me on Facebook.

To his surprise, I called him almost immediately and gave him my address so that he could mail my keepsake back to me in Southern California. I told him how moved and grateful I was for his honesty, and how much it means to me to get this treasured item back. Through FB, Jay and I became friends, and the next time I'm in Vegas I look forward to meeting him personally.

THERE'S NO MONEY THAT CAN PUT A VALUE ON SOMETHING AS PERSONAL AS A PRIVATE SCRAPBOOK

There's no money that can put a value on something as personal as a private scrapbook, which is even sweeter coming back to me at this point in my life. There were many things in that book that completely validated what I had written in my autobiography. There was even a bankbook register from 1981 that shows the most amount of money that I deposited that year was a little over $600.

For Jay, it also validated that by

listening to his gut, he did the right thing. When I called him, he admitted to always being a huge fan and said that he never dreamed that he'd be talking to me personally. My call, which cheered him, couldn't have been timelier, as he just lost his mother the week before, on July 4, and felt devastated.

I responded that I had lost my own mom on July 3 back in 1993, and suggested that perhaps our mothers had connected on the other side, and conspired to connect Jay and me. I think that gave him much-needed comfort that everything happens for a reason, and affirms the fact that we cannot ever lose our faith that miracles do happen—even through the sometimes controversial tool of social media.

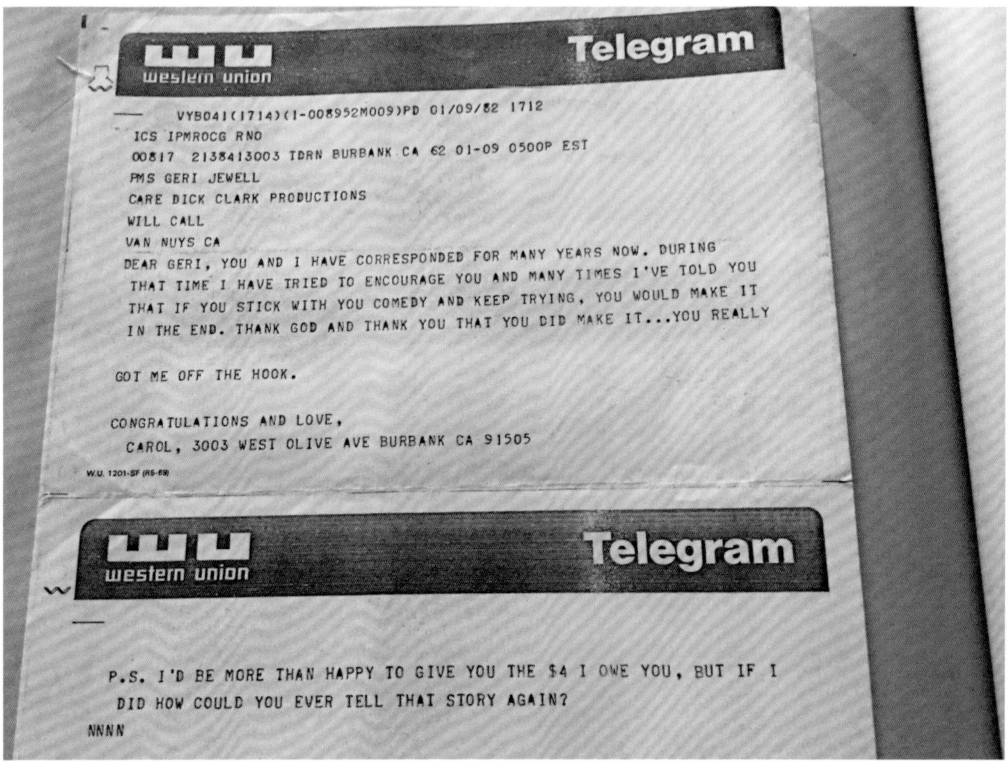

western union Telegram

VYB041(1714)(1-008952M009)PD 01/09/82 1712
ICS IPMROCG RNO
00817 2138413003 TDRN BURBANK CA 62 01-09 0500P EST
PMS GERI JEWELL
CARE DICK CLARK PRODUCTIONS
WILL CALL
VAN NUYS CA
DEAR GERI, YOU AND I HAVE CORRESPONDED FOR MANY YEARS NOW. DURING THAT TIME I HAVE TRIED TO ENCOURAGE YOU AND MANY TIMES I'VE TOLD YOU THAT IF YOU STICK WITH YOU COMEDY AND KEEP TRYING, YOU WOULD MAKE IT IN THE END. THANK GOD AND THANK YOU THAT YOU DID MAKE IT...YOU REALLY

GOT ME OFF THE HOOK.

CONGRATULATIONS AND LOVE,
CAROL, 3003 WEST OLIVE AVE BURBANK CA 91505

W.U. 1201-SF (R5-69)

western union Telegram

P.S. I'D BE MORE THAN HAPPY TO GIVE YOU THE $4 I OWE YOU, BUT IF I DID HOW COULD YOU EVER TELL THAT STORY AGAIN?
NNNN

BOOM—THERE IT IS!

Have you ever woken up and wondered how you got to be so old? I'm going to be 58 this year, and although some people say it's the new 38, that doesn't change the reality that I'm among the last of the Baby Boomer generation.

Growing up in a middle class American family allowed me to acquire cherished memories of a life that kids today will never appreciate, nor fully understand. Many of the things that shaped our lives in years gone by, are now considered to be the dinosaurs of yesterday. Meanwhile, technology speeds us through life.

Are you old enough to remember the excitement of going to a drive-in movie? Back in the day, we'd get in our jammies, fill the car with pillows and blankets, bring homemade popcorn and drive into a big lot with a huge screen at the front of it. To hear the movie, we'd hang the speaker in the window and excitedly wait for the picture show to begin. But there wasn't just one movie; we'd see a "double feature"—plus a brand-new cartoon as a prelude! This was when the cost of movie night rarely exceeded $12 and there was money left over!

On summer evenings, I remember going for rides in the family car, cruising along with no particular destination in mind. We'd crank the windows down, and let the wind caress our faces as we watched the world drift by. And of course, we'd stop for ice cream somewhere along the way. We'd arrive home, never concerned that we'd wasted a tank of gas, which was less than a $1 a gallon, or that we'd almost gotten lost at a time when a GPS system was unheard of. Even if we did get turned around on occasion, there was no anxiety; we savored the thrill of discovering a road less traveled.

WE'D CRANK THE WINDOWS DOWN, AND LET THE WIND CARESS OUR FACES AS WE WATCHED THE WORLD DRIFT BY.

In the 60's and 70's, there were no mobile or smart phones. All we had was a stupid wall phone mounted in the kitchen. It was covered with greasy hand prints and a cord that got so tightly tangled that it never stretched long enough to reach the privacy of a bedroom.

I don't even have memories of wanting to call anyone until high school. Back then, if I needed privacy, I'd ride my bike to a phone booth with a pocketful of dimes. The phone booth has largely disappeared from our lives. Think fast, where and when did you last see one? I bet you can't remember, can you?

As a child, I had a fondness for writing. In 1969, when I was 13, all I wanted for Christmas was an electric typewriter. Sure, my family owned a manual one, but having cerebral palsy made it difficult for me to use it. So I was thrilled that year when an electric typewriter appeared under the tree. Back then, it never occurred to me that the typewriter—electric or manual—would ever become extinct. The last typewriter I owned was in 1983. I donated it to Goodwill Industries and subsequently replaced it with a word processor—and then a computer!

Of course, these are only a few of the items that are no longer. There are other things that were equally important in shaping how I grew up, but I'm happy to live without them. I'm talking Hostess cupcakes, Twinkies, fruit pies, snowballs, Thomas Guide Maps and transistor radios.

Remember Earth Shoes, Sting Ray bicycles and strap on roller skates? Crackerjack boxes with prizes were actually pretty cool, or lava lamps, which never actually cast enough light in a room to read by, but then who wanted to read when you could space out in a beanbag chair and daydream?

The only high I experienced growing up was from the sugar rush of M&Ms. I would separate the different colors and put them in empty pill bottles, as if they were prescription drugs. But the truth is, I stayed on the straight and narrow, focused on someday becoming an actress and a writer. As I compose this—having exceeded so many of my daydreams—I wonder if I could have accomplished as much if I'd been distracted by today's constant pursuit of instant gratification. I probably could have, but never with the sweetness and innocence of growing up a Boomer.

I WONDER IF I COULD HAVE ACCOMPLISHED AS MUCH IF I'D BEEN DISTRACTED BY TODAY'S CONSTANT PURSUIT OF INSTANT GRATIFICATION.

NATIONAL ACADEMY OF TELEVISION ARTS AND SCIENCES

RED CARPET

There was no shortage of glitzy awards shows packed into the end of 2013 and the beginning of 2014. They all included red carpet moments where the celebrities had to walk, be vulnerable to criticism, and judged in the court of public opinion. Whether we have to walk a red carpet like the celebs and well-known athletes who've come out as gay in recent months, or those who march to a different drummer and are still wandering around on the shag carpet of the 70's—the point is that we're all trying to put our best foot forward in life, hoping that we'll be loved.

Since my *Facts of Life* years, I had to walk the red carpet at the Emmys, the American Music Awards and the Daytime Emmys, where I perceived that my colleagues and I were all striving for perfection. These days I cannot watch those few treacherous moments, from the limo to the entrance, without wondering if it's as nerve wracking an experience for that person as it was for me. I mean, to see Jennifer Lawrence trip in back-to-back Academy Award shows is just painful, because she doesn't even have cerebral palsy, like I do, so I know that easily could have been me.

MAYBE WE ALL SHOULD LIGHTEN UP AND GO EASIER ON ONE ANOTHER.

Like millions of other people, I was glued to the television watching the most recent Academy Awards. I thought it was pretty good for the most part, but when host Ellen DeGeneres passed out pizza slices to the likes of Meryl Streep, Kerry Washington and Brad Pitt, I got such a craving that I was forced to rush to the phone and order up a pie of my own. I didn't have a Pharrell Williams' Smokey the Bear hat to collect tip money as Ellen did, but my delivery guy seemed pleased nevertheless.

I thought Ellen did a good job as host. She's usually very sensitive to others, perhaps for walking the purple carpet some years earlier (coming out as gay), and taking all those hits for it. Her monologue was funny for the most part, but when she made that jab at Liza Minnelli— suggesting that the performer was not herself, but instead a male impersonating Liza Minnelli—I cringed. I'm sure Ellen's line was off the cuff, with no malicious intent, but it felt insensitive to the fact that here was Liza with her sister, Lorna, and brother, Joey, gathered together to celebrate their mother's film, The Wizard of Oz! We're talking a Hollywood classic, starring Judy Garland, and I think all three of them deserved better. Ellen didn't seize the moment to give them the proper acknowledgement. How wonderful if Liza, Lorna and Joey had been chosen to give an Oz award. Just saying that was a missed opportunity by the Academy.

Now can we talk John Travolta? Yes, he called the singer Idina Menzel by the wrong name, Adele Mazeem, and we laughed at him. It could be argued that we should be more sensitive ourselves, I mean it's been well documented that Travolta has struggled with dyslexia... And yet he's a Scientologist, and they don't acknowledge disability right? Or am I confusing him with Tom Cruise? In any case, maybe we all should lighten up and go easier on one another. I think Travolta saw the humor and humanity in the gaffe himself, and that humanity is just the part of the Oscars that most of us can relate to.

For example, Matthew McCaughey's win for Best Actor in Dallas Buyers Club showcased his amazing portrayal of aids patient Ron Woodroof. His acceptance speech, thanking God and family was beautiful, giving conservatives something to applaud. But at the same time, they could not ignore that he played the role of a man, previously homophobic, who ended up bringing a sense of humanity to the AIDS epidemic—not to mention saving many lives. My point being: Do not ignore the whole picture here; the film he was awarded for challenges us to be more educated and less prejudiced, again the vulnerability of being human.

The only films that I did not see were Woody Allen's, Blue Jasmine, and the animated film, Frozen, but now I will check out both, to catch the work of Cate Blanchett and to hear the song, "Let it Go" by Adele Mazeem, I mean Idina Mizell—although the Beatles song "Let It Be" is still tops with me.

THE IMPORTANT THING IS THAT WE SHOW UP IN LIFE. THAT'S WHAT MAKES US WINNERS!

Over the years, the red carpet will continue to be rolled out for award shows, and no matter what path each of us is on, it doesn't matter so much if we trip, flub our makeup, or wear the wrong gown or tux. The important thing is that we show up in life. That's what makes us winners!

COOKIE MONSTER

This past holiday season I was knocked down by the flu TWICE...and I had a flu shot! So, how do I feel now? I feel like the flu shot was a useless pain in the arm! I also feel that getting the flu at the end of the year was a good omen I guess, because I knew I would start the New Year being healthy. I mean, after two bouts with the flu in December, I had enough orange juice, chicken soup, Gatorade, steamed rice, flu and cold meds to win the war against any germs that were in my system and not bring them with me into 2014.

When I began to feel better the first time, I didn't feel that I had time to do the Christmas shopping that I would have, so I thought I'd make Toll House chocolate chip walnut cookies to give as gifts. I remembered how much I loved them when Mom used to make them for the holidays, and how the smell of fresh baked cookies filled the house, and the cookies filled our tummies with comfort and joy. We even left some by the fireplace for Santa Claus.

So with these warm feel good memories of home baked cookies by Mom, I set out to do the same. Went to the store to get all the ingredients, and the recipe hadn't changed much over the years, but a few things have changed dramatically—like how much everything costs! Wow, a small fortune to bake cookies from scratch now! The walnuts alone cost about $16.00 if you tripled the recipe like I did. One good thing though, flour is now pre-sifted. Yes, it's been that long since I've made cookies.

I played holiday music on the computer, ran a string of blinking colored lights over the flat screen television, and set the oven at 350. Next, I got out an electric beater that looked almost as old as an antique flour sifter and began my cookie adventure. As I kept adding more and more flour, it was getting harder and harder to beat.

Funny, I didn't seem to recall this being so much physical work, but then again, I was 30 years younger, and A LOT stronger. It got to the point where I could no longer beat it on the counter. I had to sit on the kitchen floor with the bowl between my legs, beating it from a slightly different vantage point. However, within minutes the beater was beating at a speed that wasn't even on the beater, so fast, that cookie dough went everywhere. Even my UGG boots were covered with it, looking like I had come in from walking through the snow.

WITHIN MINUTES THE BEATER WAS BEATING AT A SPEED THAT WASN'T EVEN ON THE BEATER, SO FAST, THAT COOKIE DOUGH WENT EVERYWHERE.

The beater started to smell and smoke, so I pulled the plug and tossed it in the trash. I added the chocolate chips and walnuts to the bowl of dough, put it in the fridge, turned off the oven, cleaned the kitchen, loaded the dishwasher, and washed the floor. Put my UGG boots in the freezer, took a bath and went to bed. I was exhausted!

The next morning I removed the cookie dough from the fridge and the boots from the freezer, waited patiently for them both to thaw. For the next three hours I baked cookies. Then I tasted the first home baked cookie from the oven, closed my eyes, and remembered my mom with a whole new appreciation for what she did to make the holidays so special.

I entered the new year with the resolution that I would not bake cookies again until I buy a new beater, which I have no immediate plans of doing. I will also do my cards and shopping long before December just in case I have the flu again, and I will cherish the memories I have from my childhood a little bit more—a time when there was Mayberry and no Honey Boo Boo, and when we drank water from the hose, owned a sifter and the Cookie Monster was on television, not the demon that possessed my electric beater! Happy New Year everyone.

I WILL CHERISH THE MEMORIES I HAVE FROM MY CHILDHOOD A LITTLE BIT MORE—A TIME WHEN THE COOKIE MONSTER WAS ON TELEVISION, NOT THE DEMON THAT POSSESSED MY ELECTRIC BEATER!

CONGRESS NEEDS A REBOOT

While I was born with cerebral palsy, which is considered a disability under the Americans with Disabilities Act (ADA), I feel blessed that I do not have a more tragic disability-like members of the United States Congress, who recently had trouble finding a way to keep the government running. When I was in the womb, my brain was deprived of oxygen, but the Congressional brain seems to be deprived of common sense and is amped up on a false sense of power, which led to a dysfunctional, 16-day government shutdown, and caused an estimated $24 billion in pain and suffering for hundreds of millions of people.

Is being a member of Congress recognized as a disability under the ADA? Unfortunately no, and the congresspersons themselves don't even realize how disabling their condition can be. They're all gainfully employed, own homes, and have far better health insurance than most of us could afford, even with a government subsidy. Unfortunately, this bubble can insulate them from how their conduct impacts those who do not enjoy these securities.

WE, THE PEOPLE, NEED TO DEMAND THAT OUR ELECTED REPRESENTATIVES SHOW RESPECT FOR THE CONSTITUTION OF THE UNITED STATES.

That being said, are there members of Congress who are "less disabled" than others? Of course, but those who continued to perpetuate this ridiculous shutdown definitely have a more severe case of it and should be covered under the ADA. They need to experience unemployment, go without health insurance, have their homes foreclosed upon, and be forced to apply for Social Security Disability Insurance at least three times, so they can see how the other half (three quarters? 99 percent?) lives. If they were forced to squeak by, as millions of people with disabilities do, they might be cured of their arrogance, indifference and unwillingness to acknowledge the consequences of their inaction.

If Congress were a PC computer that shut down, it would have flashed the message:

The US Government was shutdown improperly. Would you like to start again in safe mode (recommended)?

And what would be the ideal "safe mode"? I think it would be that we, the people, need to recognize that it is our country and demand that our elected representatives show respect for the Constitution of the United States. We also need to keep the damn national monuments open. I finally made it down to Little Rock, AR, and couldn't go in the Clinton Library because those bozos in Congress were asleep at the wheel.

BREATH ADDICTION

Face it: humans have addictive personalities. Our very first addiction is to breathing. I can just see myself at a 12-step meeting confessing: "My name is Geri, and I am a breath addict. I took my first breath at 8:34 a.m. on September 13, 1956, and I've been taking breaths ever since. I even breathe while I'm asleep."

In fact, our addiction to breathing is a good thing. To stop would be the death of us. So clearly some addictions are positive. I think that knowing the difference requires us to be consciously aware of our intentions as much as possible and to pay heed to what we do with each breath we take. Awareness is the most powerful gift we have to navigate our lives. We should bring that awareness to our choices, even though some decisions are more difficult to make than others.

Addictions can be positive if the intention behind them serves a higher purpose. Addiction is bad when it becomes harmful to mind, body, spirit and/or soul undermining our ability to live abundantly. If truth be known, we have to consciously choose to be happy so that life will reflect that choice back to us, allowing us greater contentment, higher self-esteem and more opportunities to honor each breath we take.

LIKE BREATHING, UNHAPPINESS IS A PART OF THE HUMAN CONDITION.

Not all of our addictions are so easily identified and even the ones that are obviously bad, such as drugs, alcohol, food, sex and gambling, often require that we hit rock bottom before we recognize that we need help. However, there is one addiction that is the supreme baddy of them all. Unfortunately many of us are unaware of the degree to which this one feeds into every other negative addiction.

Can you guess what it is? It's the addiction to unhappiness. Yep, unhappiness is an addiction. Like breathing, unhappiness is a part of the human condition. But unlike breathing, we won't die if we give up being unhappy. The problem is that we feed the addiction of unhappiness by amplifying our grievances and honing our anger. Most of us fail to see that this is something we have the power to change. We believe we are victims and expend an enormous amount of energy complaining. This is how the addiction to unhappiness grows around us like a cloying vine, choking off the joy.

So why do we not have a 12-step program for our addiction to unhappiness? If we did it would far surpass all the other 12-step programs and people would attend meetings in droves. "Hi, my name is Jose, and I am addicted to unhappiness. I first became unhappy when I was forced to share my toys with my sister, and then...and then...and then... But in 2006, I realized that I had to sober up, and stop drinking the unhappiness Kool-Aid. I've been happy now for seven years, three months and two weeks."

Unhappiness Anonymous would probably not work because unlike other 12-step programs, this one would only reinforce the addiction to unhappiness. Every time we utter past grievances, anger and despair, we tell the universe that we expect more and the universe gives us just what we expect.

So what is the prescription for our addiction to unhappiness? The path is unique for each of us, it could be getting therapy, eating properly, exercising, putting acts of kindness in motion and making daily choices that court happiness. More importantly, we must be aware of when we are slipping. Have we spoken ill of someone? Have we rehashed a time when we were victimized? Do we believe that a person or situation in our past is still harming us in the present? Are we waxing our pain to a high-gloss shine?

THOSE OF US WHO'VE BEEN ABUSED, BULLIED AND/OR HURT DEEPLY ARE MORE CHALLENGED THAN OTHERS TO AVOID REPEATING THOSE EXPERIENCES.

Those of us who've been abused, bullied and/or hurt deeply are more challenged than others to avoid repeating those experiences. Manifesting the same old-same old can become a vicious cycle and we might not think to interrupt it because we aren't surprised when we encounter a situation that makes us unhappy again. Primarily because the scenario is so familiar, on some psychic and unconscious level, we are co-creating what we have experienced in the past.

The prescription, therefore, demands that we become aware of when we are slipping into unhappiness and quickly counter that misstep with positive action, thought or comment. The more we do this, the easier it becomes to truly experience happiness. It takes daily effort to achieve, but the good news is that the process of embracing happiness is attainable to us all.

We can't control other people's choices, or the negative things that can happen to anyone from time to time, but we can control our reactions and remain aware of how they feed into our unhappiness addiction. Just remember though, that it takes courage to let go of our damaging patterns. It's a lifelong process and I urge everyone who struggles with the effect of this destructive behavior to summon the will to move forward, find inspiration and embrace the things that make you happy. Go for it. I dare you!

IT TAKES
COURAGE TO
LET GO OF OUR
DAMAGING
PATTERNS.

PET POWER

From the day I came home from the hospital as a newborn in 1956, my family's had pets. Back then it was a gold German Shepherd named Kim. In my first two years, she was as much a part of our household as my parents or two older brothers. Though Kim was technically not my sister, she was my protector and friend.

As I maneuvered my little walker, I held onto her ear. Incredibly patient, she moved with me, never pulling away. She slept nearby and growled at anyone who tried to get too close.

When our beloved Kim was taken from us tragically, I lost a best friend and our whole family grieved her passing.

Over the years, I've found living with animals to be a privilege, whether they be pets, service animals, or creatures that live outdoors and simply stop in to visit.

After Kim's death, we got two cats, Gunsmoke and Maverick. And then, when I was a little older, we got another German Shepherd that we named Kelly. Truthfully, without the emotional bond I formed with that four-footed friend, I would have been very lonely.

THEY PROVIDED LIGHT WHEN THERE WAS DARKNESS, JOY WHEN THERE WAS DESPAIR.

Later our family acquired a couple of parakeets, Angel and Pepe; two lizards, Larry and Leonard; as well as a desert turtle named Timothy. Timothy just walked up our driveway one day and stayed for 14 years. When Timothy laid an egg, we had to rename her Timothy Jean, all things considered. One day, out of the blue, our slow-walking buddy wandered away just as mysteriously as she'd arrived.

In the 1980's, I rescued a cat named Lady. She also became a best friend, giving me comfort as I learned how to survive in Hollywood. She even posed with me in a photo for Cosmopolitan magazine.

Then I acquired four Japanese Bobtail cats, which were by my side for 18 years. They provided light when there was darkness, joy when there was despair and hope when I needed a good reason to keep on keeping on.

Now, I have two more Japanese Bobtails: Harry and Juliet. Harry is a 10-yearold retired show cat; he loves to sit on my lap and watch retro TV. He also gets a kick out of that cat food commercial from the 70's with the irritating "Meow Meow Meow Meow" song.

Juliet is a diva with more issues than the Kardashians! Although it was a rescue kitty named Joey, who sat on my printer, pressed the "start button, and took a photo of his own butt-his cat scan, it was Juliet who sat on my head meowing up a storm while zooming into an International Disability Conference from the United Nations!

I've rarely been without a pet and when I have, I've longed for one in the back of my mind. Pets are not just great huggers, they can improve your health by lowering your blood pressure, making you feel less alone, getting you out for a walk to slim your waistline and even helping you attract a new friend or mate. So by all means, if you've been longing for a pet in the back of your mind, consider adopting a little furry son or daughter.

PAPER OR PLASTIC

With the bans on single plastic bag use in some of California's grocery stores, other states will also be following the trend, making it illegal, beginning January 2013, to pack your produce in plastic. Why such drastic measures on the use of plastic bags? It is all in the name of saving the environment, being eco-friendly and forcing us to use the more easily recyclable, 15-cent paper bag or the reusable dollar priced bags the stores offer every time we grocery shop.

So why are so many people so cranky and upset over this change that may help our planet to survive? The number one reason is simply because we hate change; especially when we have been doing something one way for such a long time. The second reason is because we resent having to pay 15 cents for paper, or a dollar for the reusable eco-friendly bags.

But let's be honest, there are yet other reasons that we are irked by this inconvenience—reasons that we may not care to admit (except maybe to our therapist). It is upsetting that we will no longer be able to have readily available plastic bags to toss out the cat litter or dog poop or line that little wastebasket in the bathroom. But, I think there is another reason we are having trouble making the change.

When we do try to do our part to save the environment by paying a dollar for reusable bags, nine times out of ten, we forget to bring them into the store with us when we go shopping. Therefore, we end up buying more dollar-priced bags, and before we know it, we have enough eco-friendly bags to fill a Mini Cooper! So, I think it is time to get more innovative in creating additional uses for these bags that are so often forgotten.

Here are a few things I have thought of that I will share with you for no charge at all, because I'm tired of all the griping from you "plastic-bag dependents." I have discovered that they are great for carry-on items when traveling, trick or treat bags on Halloween, shoe storage in small closets and even gift bags for holidays and birthdays. They can be decorated for any occasion, and people will think it was thoughtful that you cared enough to give them an eco-friendly grocery

GOOD HABITS HAVE TO BE FORMED, AND WITH REPETITION, THEY WILL BECOME SECOND NATURE.

bag, as opposed to using paper that took the life of a tree. They are also useful for making doll clothes and fabulous for moving!

However, there is still the issue of forgetting the bags on the kitchen table where we left them as a reminder, and then we end up having to buy yet another bag. Good habits have to be formed, and with repetition, they will become second nature. Simply put a post-it on the dashboard that says: Don't forget the reusable bags. If you still forget them, then tell the cashier that you would like the groceries to be put in your shopping cart without being bagged. They cannot refuse, because you paid for the groceries. Just make sure you hold on to your receipt. So stop whining, and stop making your bags emotional baggage. Get smart, get creative and bag the bad attitude.

SO STOP WHINING,
AND STOP
MAKING YOUR
BAGS EMOTIONAL
BAGGAGE.

LAST MINUTE 2013 RESOLUTIONS

If the world had ended in 2012 as scheduled, we'd all be off the hook from making New Year's resolutions. But as I'm sure you've heard by now, the world kept on turning, and here we are in 2013. If you're like me, you rang in the year with at least one resolution, possibly more.

Now, we all know this is a mind game: Thinking that by striking a conscious deal with ourselves, we'll honor it. Unfortunately, there's usually a flaw in this type of "deal," mainly because of whom we made the deal with—and because our resolutions are unrealistic and therefore hard to keep.

Bottom line, we want to feel better about ourselves by honoring our commitments—even if they are left over from 2012. So if the goal is to feel better, and have greater self-esteem, then why do we repeatedly make resolutions that, two months later, fall off our radar?

ONE OF MY RESOLUTIONS WAS TO BE SO SWEET TO AN ANNOYING TELEMARKETER THAT HE'D NEVER WANT TO CALL ME AGAIN.

Okay, I imagine there's a small percentage of people who do follow through on their resolutions, but the rest of us 95 percenters are skofflaws. Remember the definition of insanity: Doing the same thing over and over again, but expecting different results. That makes the vast majority of us as nutty as peanut butter.

So what's the solution to this annual resolution wipeout? First, we cannot make formal resolutions at all, because that leads to failure. We can only make "fun" resolutions with ourselves, guaranteeing greater successes, creating better self-esteem and enabling us to accomplish bigger things all year long. Fun resolutions act as a bridge between where we are now and where we want to be.

As of this writing, I've kept the resolutions I made on New Year's Eve, and there's no sign that I'm going to go back on them. One was to be so sweet to an annoying telemarketer that he'd never want to call me again. My opportunity came up a few days ago. I told the guy that I was not interested in his product, but that it was so kind of him to call me. I asked if he'd seen any good movies lately. He was silent. Then I asked him if he had seen Argo. He said no, so I told him what a wonderful film it was-in intimate detail. When he said he had to go, I asked him if he'd seen

Lincoln... He said he had, but had to get back to work. I told him how awful it was that he just couldn't call up and have a nice chat with all the strangers on his list, and by the way did he have any pets. That's when he hung up. Resolution kept!

Another handy resolution is to give yourself permission to make up a new resolution on the spot—any day, any time—just so long as it's this year. That way, if you wish to give yourself a new one to try, there's no guilt residue for not having made it on New Year's Eve. If you are on Facebook, for instance, you could agree to place a heart on the timeline of at least five of your friends, letting them know that they're thought of and loved. To create a heart, press < and 3, putting them together will create a heart.

You could offer to volunteer at a senior citizen's home once a month. Seniors love company, and often have a wealth of wisdom to share. One resolution many of us make is to save money, but a fun one is to give away pennies. Leave a handful in waiting rooms, on sidewalks or park benches. Why? Because then you co-created "pennies from Heaven" for someone.

And last, but not least—read at least one new book a month, and then go online and write a review for the author. To start, consider reading my autobiography, *I'm Walking as Straight as I Can*—and then writing a review on Amazon and Barnes and Noble.com. Now, don't you feel better about yourself already?

ANOTHER HANDY RESOLUTION IS TO GIVE YOURSELF PERMISSION TO MAKE UP A NEW RESOLUTION ON THE SPOT.

SPRING INTO ACTION

It's that time of year again, the vernal equinox, when night and day are nearly the same length. In Latin, *ver* means "spring" and *equinox* means "equal night." And while there's a fall equinox, only in spring does the sun cross the equator moving northward, on the up, you might say.

This time of year means different things to different people. For example, college students, who spend the week between terms partying, call it Spring Break; while Christians think more along the lines of the resurrection of Christ. Jews celebrate Passover, while florists rejoice at the sudden surge of flower sales.

Of course, children become obsessed with candy-filled Easter baskets, colored eggs and a mystical bunny that hides eggs for them to hunt; while those with hay fever are basket cases, thinking only of Claritin and Benadryl.

All versions of spring are valid, including spring cleaning and spring fever. The former may mean cleaning your home top to bottom, getting your taxes done or reevaluating your Facebook friend list, and deleting those people you can't remember "friending" in the first place.

Spring fever may show up as listlessness, restlessness, loss of appetite, intense nervous excitement and insomnia. But those could just be symptoms of wanting desperately for summer to arrive.

SEE WHAT MIGHT BE POKING YOU AND CAUSING DISCOMFORT, AND LET IT GO.

Regardless of what vernal equinox means to each of us, one constant is that winter is its prelude. In spring, we temporarily say goodbye to cold weather and watch the snowmen melt, their carrot noses nibbled by rabbits that may or may not be related to the mystical egg-hiding bunny.

In every season, we should greet the day with a spring in our step, springing forward with optimism and hope.

We should spring into action when help is needed, and use each day as a springboard to launch us closer to our dreams. Remember, an attitude of gratitude goes a long way in winter, spring, summer and fall.

If your mattress springs poke you, turn it over to see if it feels any better. If not, chuck the thing. Same with your life: See what might be poking you and causing discomfort, and let it go, like the soft petals of a dandelion head in a March wind.

Happy spring everyone!

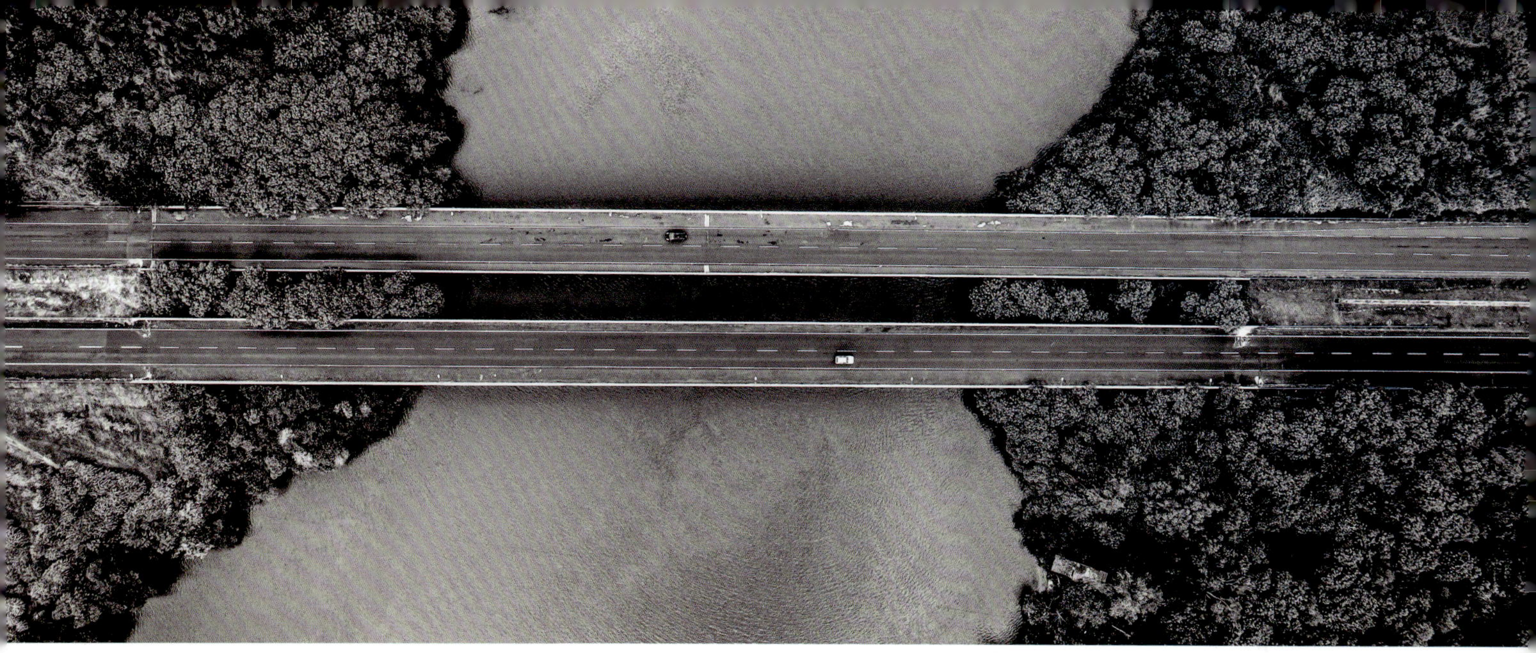

NEXT EXIT, JOY

It's so unfortunate that today's society makes it difficult to take a breather. Our brains are multi-tasked to the max and simple things that give us joy are oftentimes overrun by our obsession with surviving. Our minds become a mangled maze of freeways and toll roads with no off ramps or rest areas. This must stop! We have to consciously create a Joy Exit at least three times a day or happiness may elude us.

Staying in hamster-wheel mode provokes some of us to become dependent on artificial joy—pleasures found outside of ourselves such as drugs, alcohol, food, sex or gambling. We shift into higher and higher gears, maintaining unsustainable speeds, rarely stopping because we are so wrapped up in checking off the mileposts. Chronic and other killer conditions may loom just ahead.

Sometimes we slow down but only because traffic is bumper to bumper, or there are tolls where we pause briefly to take care of such responsibilities as our monthly bills, taxes, dental and medical expenses. Then we accelerate again, reeling with our need to jam it all in. We try to manage our anger and frustration at having no time for ourselves, even as our anxieties become unmanageable and end up feeding into our survival rage. I wonder if those anxieties inflame our outbreaks of violence towards one another.

More than ever, we need a Joy Exit. At least three times a day, we need to practice self-care and take ourselves out of the race. The first step is to consciously want to experience real happiness. The second is to replace our mental gearshift with a joystick. Shifting into joy mode enables us to find fulfillment in our lives, regardless of our challenges to survive. Every time we shift gears and opt for the Joy Exit, we consciously create healing moments of happiness.

AT LEAST THREE TIMES A DAY, WE NEED TO PRACTICE SELF-CARE AND TAKE OURSELVES OUT OF THE RACE.

Look for—or create in your mind—a "Joy Exit Ahead" sign. Do not blow past these important road markers because once you do, the distance between them may become greater.

Even in serious situations, you can create a Joy Exit. Following my neck surgery, I had to wear a brace from my neck down to my torso. I was in agony physically, emotionally, psychologically and spiritually. But I decided to shift the joystick and hang a toy man-eating shark, a Tinky Winky doll, a pink eraser and a small "Do Not Enter" sign on the front of the brace. When people looked at me, they didn't get sad, they laughed—creating a shared moment of amusement and joy. Their laughter lifted my spirits and moved me closer to my recovery.

Here are some Joy Exits that you can take at any time: smile at someone; soak in a bubble bath; read a good book (including mine); laugh with family and friends; take in the glorious wonders of nature; sing in the shower; dance in the rain; help someone in need; listen to music that opens your heart; and take time to smell the posies. When you take Joy Exits, you accelerate towards happiness.

GERI JEWELL RESUMÉ

SAG-AFTRA ***HAIR**: Light brown* ***EYES**: Blue* ***WEBSITE**: gerijewell.com*

FILM:

Hemispheres: A Documentary on Cerebral Palsy	Herself	
Night of the White Pants	Supporting	Dir: Amy Talkington
Nice Dreams	Supporting	Dir:Thomas Chong

MOVIE OF THE WEEK:

Two of a Kind	Supporting	Dir: Roger Young CBS

TELEVISION:

The Deadwood Movie	Jewel	HBO
Carol of the Bells	Sister Gloria	Netflex
The Home & Family Show	Herself	Hallmark
The Doctors	Herself	Syndication
Archive of American Television	Herself	PBS
Glee	Studio Exec.	FOX
Alcatraz	Geri Tiller	FOX
After Lately	Herself	E!
2011 TV LAND AWARDS	Herself	TV Land
Strong Medicine	Guest Star	Lifetime
Deadwood	Jewel (Recurring 23 ep.)	HBO
Biography: The Facts of Life	Herself	NBC
The Young & Restless	Recurring	CBS
E! True Hollywood Story	Herself	E! Entertainment
21 Jump Street	Guest Star/Ep. Writer	FOX
On Stage America	Herself	
The Facts of Life	Cousin Geri/Recurring (12 eps.)	NBC
I Love Liberty	Herself	
Sesame Street	Herself	PBS
Wisecracks	Herself	
The Mo Show	Herself	Syndicated
Phil Donahue	Herself	Syndicated
Larry King Live	Herself	CNN
Secret Life of the Very Young	Herself	W/ John Ritter

TRAINING:

Acting Classes	Corey Allen
Acting Classes	Estelle Harmon

ADDITIONAL RECENT SHOWS:

2 episodes of *History of the Sitcom*, CNN
Facts of Life: Behind Closed Doors, Reelz TV

ABOUT THE AUTHOR

GERI JEWELL started her career as a stand-up comic, and is best known for her role as "Cousin Geri" on the ground-breaking sitcom NBC's *The Facts of Life,* and a reoccurring role in HBO's *Deadwood.* Geri has appeared on numerous comedy cable shows such as A&E's *Evening at the Improv*, VHI's *Spotlight*, and Comedy Central.

She appeared in the Emmy® Award-winning movie *Two of a Kind*, with George Burns and Robby Benson. She has also appeared in *I Love Liberty, 21 Jump Street, Sesame Street, The New Adventures of Lassie, Strong Medicine, The Young and the Restless, Alcatraz* and *Glee*. She co-starred in the film *Night of the White Pants* with Tom Wilkinson. Most recently co-starred in HBO's *Deadwood: The Movie*, and a cameo appearance in the movie *Carol of the Bells*.

Geri's autobiography, *I'm Walking as Straight as I Can* received the 2012 Gold Award by the Independent Publishers for Best Memoir. She also wrote a bi-monthly column for the award winning magazine *Ability*.

All in all, Geri is enjoying a thriving career. She has been the recipient of many awards, including the 1992 Founders Award, the 2005 Independent Living Legacy Award, and the 2006 Victory award. She also received the 2013 Golden Halo Award, and the 2013 UCP Life Without Limits Award.

She is currently starring and producing an upcoming documentary, *My Next Breath*.